Cranmer's immense contribution to Anglican doctrine and practice, especially in his liturgical output and limpid language, is a legacy fast being squandered. With it, commitment to orthodoxy and the biblical gospel is correspondingly eroded. Active retrieval of Cranmer's commitment to the doctrine of the Trinity, with its varied outworking, is imperative. In this excellent little book Chris Young points the way forward.

Revd Dr Robert Letham, Senior Research Fellow, Union School of Theology

Latimer Studies 90

Thomas Cranmer and 'Of Faith in the Holy Trinity'

Chris Young

The Latimer Trust

Acknowledgements

I would like to thank Professor Robert Letham for giving his time and expertise in reading this book, and for his gracious and helpful comments. I am also very grateful to family, friends and colleagues who read the draft and made extremely valuable suggestions. Most of all, as Cranmer would always have us remember, 'Glory be to the Father, and to the Son, and to the Holy Ghost. As it was in the beginning, is now, and ever shall be: world without end. Amen.'

Contents

1. Introduction: Thomas Cranmer and 'Of Faith in the Holy Trinity'

> There is but one living and true God, everlasting, without body, parts or passions, of infinite power, wisdom and goodness, the maker and preserver of all things both visible and invisible. And in Unity of this Godhead there be three persons, of one substance, power and eternity, the Father, the Son and the Holy Ghost.

This article, *Of Faith in the Holy Trinity,* is the first of Archbishop Thomas Cranmer's *Forty-Two Articles of Religion.*[1] Finalised in 1553, at the very height of the English Reformation under Edward VI, the Articles – along with the 1552 *Book of Common Prayer* – represent Cranmer's fullest expression of Protestant theology.[2]

Much has been written on Cranmer's Reformation theology, and much has been written about other Reformers' theologies of the Trinity. But Cranmer's own doctrine of the Trinity has received little real attention. Biographies of Cranmer touch lightly on the subject, while historical-theological treatments of the Trinity rarely discuss Cranmer in any great detail. There are perhaps reasons for this: it is true that Cranmer did not write specifically or extensively on the subject, as other Reformers did (Calvin, for instance, in his *Institutes*). It is also true that the doctrine of the Trinity was not a major theological battle ground for Cranmer. On the subject of the three divine Persons, the Reformers were broadly in agreement with Rome.

However, while others may have written more directly on the Trinity and contributed more to the development of the doctrine, it is Cranmer who,

---

[1] Gerald Bray, ed., *Documents of the English Reformation* (Cambridge: James Clarke & Co, 1994), 285 (modernised spellings original). All quotations from the 1553 Articles are from this immensely useful anthology. The finalised *Forty-Two Articles* 'were promulgated on 19 June 1553, and clergy were instructed to subscribe to them', 284. Tragically, Edward VI died early the next month, and the Articles were dropped by Queen Mary. However, under Elizabeth I, they were revised into the Thirty-Nine Articles that are now so widely known. Cranmer, 1489–1556, was Archbishop of Canterbury 1533–55.

[2] Bray even comments: 'When Cranmer produced the 1553 edition, it was the most advanced systematization of Protestant theology then in existence anywhere.' (*Documents*, 284.)

through his liturgy, has imprinted Trinitarian truth on the hearts and minds of the English-speaking world. Still today, millions of believers regularly articulate Cranmer's theology of the triune God (whether or not they are conscious that that is what they are doing). Given the astonishingly powerful role that Cranmer's liturgy has played – and continues to play – in the spiritual formation of so many, his theology of the Trinity surely merits closer examination and appreciation.

In this short book, I hope to take a step towards that goal, recognising that there is always more that could be said. We will examine Cranmer's understanding of the Trinity, noting his debt both to those who had gone before (especially the Church Fathers) and to his contemporaries. We will see his theology emerge in several of his works, most especially in his public, corporate expression of Reformed doctrine: the deeply Trinitarian liturgy of the 1552 *Book of Common Prayer* (hereafter, *BCP*).[3] I will conclude with a number of reflections on Cranmer's subsequent influence on the Anglican (and wider) world in this area of doctrine, noting finally some areas of concern and application for Anglicans today.[4]

---

[3] The 1552 *BCP* is available online: http://justus.anglican.org/resources/bcp/1552/BCP_1552.htm. Spelling and punctuation has been modernised.

[4] We should note that the word 'Anglican' would have been alien to Cranmer, as it originates from the nineteenth century (see Mark Chapman, *Anglican Theology* (London: T&T Clark, 2012), 1–9), but it is a useful shorthand.

2. Cranmer's Trinitarian Roots

First and foremost, Cranmer was a man who sought to root all his theology in the Holy Scriptures: hence the popular saying that the *BCP* is 'the Bible arranged for worship'.[1] However, Cranmer made no claim to be writing in a theological vacuum. He was profoundly and avowedly influenced by others. His personal library contained works by Irenaeus, Augustine, Athanasius, the Cappadocians, Peter Lombard, John Wycliffe, Thomas Aquinas, Jan Huss, Erasmus, Luther and Melanchthon (to name but a few).[2] Cranmer also had a large collection of notebooks written in his own hand, 'Consisting of extensive quotations from leading theological authorities'.[3] As we shall see, he worked closely with two other leading Reformers on the *BCP*. Here we briefly note a number of significant influences on Cranmer's Trinitarian theology.

The Church Fathers

As J. I. Packer notes, 'Cranmer held that the Fathers had, on the whole, been faithful expositors of the biblical faith, and that it was only since the twelfth century that the church had fallen into substantial error.'[4] Like all his fellow Reformers, Cranmer owed a great deal to the theologians of the early church, and freely acknowledged the fact. A striking proof of this is found in the 1538 *Thirteen Articles of Religion*, one of the *Forty-Two*'s predecessors. Article I is entitled *The Unity of God and the Trinity of Persons*, and runs thus:

---

[1] We shall later consider – from a Trinitarian perspective – Cranmer's theology of Scripture itself.

[2] The contents, history and uses of Cranmer's library are discussed by D. G. Selwyn, 'Cranmer's Library: Its Potential for Reformation Studies,' in *Thomas Cranmer: Churchman and Scholar*, ed. Paul Ayris and David Selwyn (Woodbridge: Boydell, 1993), 39–72.

[3] Ashley Null, *Cranmer's Doctrine of Repentance: Renewing the Power to Love* (Oxford: Oxford University Press, 2000; repr., 2010), 254. Dr Null has dubbed this collection 'Cranmer's Great Commonplaces' and discusses them at length, 254–69. He is currently preparing the first full English edition, which will no doubt yield fresh insights into Cranmer's understanding of the Trinity.

[4] J. I. Packer, 'Thomas Cranmer's Catholic Theology,' in *Honouring the People of God*, vol. 4 of *The Collected Shorter Writings of J. I. Packer* (Carlisle: Paternoster, 1999), 237.

Concerning the unity of the divine essence and the three persons, we hold the decree of the Council of Nicaea to be true and without any doubt to be believed, viz. that there is one divine essence which is both called and is God, eternal, incorporeal, indivisible, of immense power, wisdom and goodness, creator and preserver of all things visible and invisible, and yet there are three persons of the same essence and power, coeternal, Father, Son and Holy Spirit; and we use the name Person in the same sense as it was used by the Church Fathers, i.e. as signifying not a part or a quality in another being, but what subsists in itself. We condemn all the heresies which have arisen against this article, e.g. the Manichees, who posited two principles, one good and one evil; likewise the Valentinians, Arians, Eunomians, Muslims and all like them. We also condemn the Adoptionists, ancient and modern, who argue that there is only one person, and cleverly and impiously prate that the Word and the Holy Spirit are not distinct persons, but that the Word is just a verbal utterance and the Spirit just a movement created in things.[5]

Understandably, this article was significantly shortened for later versions of the Articles, but it does make Cranmer's attitude towards the Fathers' theology of the Trinity very clear. This same appreciation would show itself in the inclusion of the Apostles' Creed and the *Te Deum* in the Order for Morning Prayer, the Apostles' Creed again (or, on certain days, the Athanasian Creed) in the Order for Evening Prayer, and the Nicene Creed in the Order for Holy Communion: all these credal statements were products of the early church, and of course are clearly and deliberately Trinitarian in scope.[6] There is a virtually endless amount that could be said about the Fathers' teaching on the

---

[5] In Bray, *Documents*, 185. 'These Articles were composed... by Archbishop Cranmer. They... never had any official status, but they are of great interest because of what they reveal about Cranmer's links with Lutheranism', 184.
[6] In the case of the Apostles' Creed, it was Cranmer's own translation: Diarmaid MacCulloch, *Thomas Cranmer: A Life* (New Haven: Yale University Press, 1996), 209. In the 1662 *BCP*, both Morning and Evening Prayer end with the words of the Grace (2 Corinthians 13:14), but this was a later addition (although it is hard to see Cranmer having much of an objection to it!).

Trinity, but here it is important to note just how deep Cranmer's debt was to them on this – and every other – theological issue.

Medieval Theology

It is well documented that, in composing his prayer books, Cranmer happily made use of existing medieval liturgy.[7] 'Like all the reformers, Zwingli and Calvin no less than Luther or a later Anglican like Jewel, Cranmer saw in the reformation a return to catholicity, not a flight from it.'[8] The task, then, was to *reform* the church by ridding it of the errors of medieval Catholicism, but also by retaining what was useful and true to the historic faith, as proved from the Scriptures. It was into this latter category that the doctrine of the Trinity fell: on this subject, there was substantial agreement between the leading Reformers and their Roman Catholic counterparts.[9] Indeed, both the Reformers and the Roman theologians were equally zealous to protect the orthodox Trinitarian faith: 'The subtleties of radical [Trinitarian] belief rarely interested evangelicals, who were outraged by any challenge to the package of Christian ideas (as much as Catholic traditionalists) they had inherited from Christian history.'[10] Therefore it is not strange that we can detect the influence of, for example, Thomas Aquinas on

---

[7] For a helpful introduction to Medieval liturgy and its subsequent influence on the Reformation in England, see G. J. Cuming, *A History of Anglican Liturgy*, 2nd ed. (London: Macmillan, 1982), 1–86. For a useful essay on Cranmer's liturgical composition, see B. D. Spinks, 'Treasures Old and New: a look at some of Thomas Cranmer's methods of liturgical compilation,' in Ayris and Selwyn, *Thomas Cranmer: Churchman and Scholar*, 175–88. The sources for Cranmer's prayer books are also discussed by MacCulloch, *Cranmer*, 413–21. In 1915, the scholar F. E. Brightman produced an enormous work of comparison between the Prayer Books of 1549, 1552 and 1662. He also noted, where possible, pre-Reformation sources. This is still a valuable resource: F. E. Brightman, *The English Rite: Being a Synopsis of the Sources and Revisions of the Book of Common Prayer*, 2 vols (London: Rivingtons, 1915).

[8] Geoffrey W. Bromiley, 'Tradition and Traditions in Thomas Cranmer,' *Anglican and Episcopal History* 59 (1990): 473.

[9] Although of course we should note that one cannot separate the doctrine of the Trinity from other doctrines: while the Reformers and Rome generally agreed on subjects like essence, persons and unity in the Godhead, their application of these realities to (for instance) justification or the Lord's Supper diverged significantly.

[10] MacCulloch, *Cranmer*, 145. Note also Robert Letham's comment in a similar vein: 'Rome's leading contemporary apologist, Robert Bellarmine... recognises that in terms of the classic Trinitarian dogma, Calvin is orthodox.' Robert

Cranmer's understanding of the persons of the Trinity.[11] Nor are we surprised to find that in the 1552 *Prayer Book* – which saw the most drastic removal of erroneous Roman Catholic doctrine – the Trinitarian elements are essentially unchanged from previous editions.

We may illustrate this with an example from the Sarum Rite, one of the significant sources for Cranmer's liturgy. Here is the opening collect (for purity) from the Sarum Mass:

> *Deus, cui omne cor patet et omnis voluntas loquitur, et quem nullum latet secretum, purifica per infusionem Sancti Spiritus cogitationes cordis nostri, ut te perfecte diligere et digne laudare mereamur. Per Dominum nostrum Jesum Christum, Qui tecum vivit et regnat, in unitate ejusdem Spiritus Sancti, per omnia sæcula sæculorum.* Amen.[12]

Cranmer included this prayer, in its now famous English form, at the beginning of The Order for Administration of Holy Communion: 'Almighty God, unto whom all hearts be open, all desires known, and from whom no secrets are hid: cleanse the thoughts of our hearts by the inspiration of thy Holy Spirit, that we may perfectly love thee, and worthily magnify thy holy name: through Christ our Lord. Amen.'[13] By this point, Cranmer had expunged from his liturgy all venerations of the Virgin Mary, all prayers for the dead, and any suspicion of human merit. But this beautifully Trinitarian prayer was left virtually

---

Letham, *The Holy Trinity: In Scripture, Theology, History and Worship*, rev. and enl. ed. (Phillipsburg, N.J.: P&R, 2019), 298.

[11] However, we should note that with Calvin, 'one is immediately struck by an obvious difference from Aquinas... Calvin presents a biblically-based exposition in straightforward language that largely avoids philosophical terminology.' Letham, *The Holy Trinity*, 293. Thus while the Trinitarianism of Aquinas and Calvin has much in agreement, their theological methods are very different. Cranmer would agree with Calvin's direct, Scriptural approach: his reason for including the Trinitarian Creeds was that 'they may certainly be proved by certain warrants of Holy Scripture' (Article VII of Forty-Two, *Of the Three Creeds*, in Bray, *Documents, 289*). He was also insistent on intelligible language: Article XXV of Forty-Two is entitled *Men must speak in the Congregation in such Tongue as the People understandeth* (*Documents, 298*).

[12] Some versions of this prayer end simply with 'Per Christum'. This Latin version of the Sarum Mass, with a somewhat biased English translation, is available online: http://justus.anglican.org/resources/bcp/Sarum/index.htm.

[13] The longer ending of the Latin prayer, 'Who liveth and reigneth with thee...' found its place in many other prayers in the *BCP*.

untouched, save the translation into the vernacular.[14] This proves to be a consistent pattern.[15]

Fellow Reformers

The leading Reformers themselves did not disagree in any major way over the Trinity (which was certainly not the case when it came to the Eucharist!). Cranmer was very much indebted to his Reformation contemporaries: the 1553 Article *Of Faith in the Holy Trinity* – a revision of the 1538 article quoted above – 'is mainly drawn from the First Article of the Confession of Augsburg, 1530'.[16] Cranmer corresponded with his fellow Reformers overseas, including Osiander, Melanchthon, Luther and Calvin.[17] Naturally, Cranmer dealt closely with his English colleagues, among whom he was particularly close to Latimer and Ridley. The influence of Tyndale was also keenly felt in Cranmer's England. Two continental Reformers in particular played a significant part in the composition and revision of the Edwardian Prayer Books: Martin Bucer and Peter Martyr Vermigli.[18] While Cranmer remained

---

[14] MacCulloch, *Cranmer*, 418–19, discusses another familiar collect utilised by Cranmer that had its origins in the Sarum Rite: the (once again) clearly Trinitarian Collect for Peace at Evensong.

[15] MacCulloch records how during the drafting of the *Thirteen Articles* in 1538, there was easy agreement on the 'relatively uncontroversial drafts on the nature of God, original sin, and the two natures of Christ...' It was only when they began to discuss justification that there were 'bitter disagreements' (*Cranmer*, 217).

[16] W. H. Griffith Thomas, *The Principles of Theology: An Introduction to the Thirty-Nine Articles*, 6th rev. ed. (Vine Books: London, 1978), 3. The Augsburg Confession was 'drawn up by Melanchthon and Luther', xxx. The Augsburg Confession may be viewed at: https://bookofconcord.org/augsburg-confession/.

[17] In 1552, Cranmer wrote to Calvin (and others) proposing a council of Reformers, which sadly never happened: MacCulloch, *Cranmer*, 518–19. However, if it had, surely they would have discussed – and rejoiced in – the Trinity together. Note MacCulloch's caution against over-emphasising Calvin's influence on the English Reformation: '[Calvin] was respected by his English counterparts, but not in any sense central to their thinking', (*Cranmer*, 428).

[18] Indeed, Stephen Gardiner (the bishop of Winchester, and one of Cranmer's most notable opponents) brazenly accused Cranmer of being little more than a translator of Vermigli. See John Edmund Cox, ed., *Writings and Disputations of Thomas Cranmer, Archbishop of Canterbury, Martyr, 1556, Relative to the Sacrament of the Lord's Supper* (Cambridge: Cambridge University Press, 1844), 195. (This volume was compiled for the Parker Society, and, along with

the principle author and orchestrator, 'The opinions of both Bucer and Martyr very significantly influenced the revisions of the [1549] Prayer Book.'[19] Both men spent a number of years in England, and 'Martyr was actually staying with Cranmer during the preparation of the final drafts of the [1549] Prayer Book... Bucer was later asked to criticize the book for revision'.[20] While the main area of (not always unanimous) theological discussion between the three men was the Eucharist, no doubt the subject of the Trinity featured also: it is certainly a common theme in Vermigli's own writings.

A striking insight into Vermigli's Trinitarian theology is found in his commentary on the books of Kings, in which he argues that bishops may be considered as first in order without being superior in person or power. This is in contrast to the Roman Catholic understanding of the supremacy of the Pope.

> ...in the most holy Trinity... the person of the Father is first with respect to order. It does not follow from this, however, that the Son and the Holy Spirit are lesser than Him or to be subject to Him, as if they did not have just as much divinity, since they are co-essential and consubstantial with Him. Therefore, he can be given the first place of order without the first place of power, which these [Papists] so greatly pretend.'[21]

Thus, based on relations within the Trinity, a bishop in the church may be considered as a ministerial *primus inter pares*. We do not know whether Cranmer agreed with his fellow episcopalian on this particular justification for bishops. However, given that the two men worked together in the early 1550s on the reform of English canon law, it is within the bounds of possibility that they discussed the nature

---

its companion – John Edmund Cox, ed., *Miscellaneous Writings and Letters of Thomas Cranmer* (Cambridge: Cambridge University Press, 1846) – collected together the majority of Cranmer's works. The two volumes shall be referred to respectively as Cox, *Works 1* and Cox, *Works 2*.)

[19] MacCulloch, *Cranmer*, 505.

[20] MacCulloch, *Cranmer*, 416.

[21] This quotation comes from Vermigli's commentary on 1 Kings 12, written in Zurich, some years after his sojourn in England. Peter Martyr Vermigli, *Melachim Id est, Regum Libri Duo Posteriores* (Zurich, 1566), 100b. Quoted by Eric Parker, 'Vermigli on Episcopacy,' unpublished, square brackets original.

of episcopacy from this angle – an intriguing thought.[22] Given their interaction with one another, and their shared theological heritage, we should expect to see significant agreement between Cranmer's writings and those of the other Reformers on subject of the Trinity.

We now move on to consider Cranmer's Trinitarian theology in greater detail.

---

[22] The reform of English canon law was drawn up by a committee including Cranmer, Vermigli and others. It was never passed into law. After the reign of Mary, it was rediscovered, edited and published by John Foxe in 1571. It was he who christened it the *Reformatio Legum Ecclesiasticarum*. For an overview, see MacCulloch, *Cranmer*, 500–4. We shall further refer to the *Reformatio* below.

3. Cranmer's Trinitarian Theology

Cranmer never wrote specifically at length on issues of divine substance, divine persons or divine relations. However, that is not to say that he did not affirm the orthodox position of the Church on these matters: the Articles make this very clear. Trinitarian realities are also 'dissolved' into his liturgy – in much the same way as they are 'dissolved' into the Scriptures – so that the entire shape and flavour of the *BCP* is Trinitarian. We imbibe Trinitarian truth as we recite Cranmer's prayers. At times, the Trinity comes clearly and brilliantly to the fore. So, if we study the *BCP* in detail, we find a very carefully expressed, fully orthodox theology of the triune God. Here we shall consider something of what Cranmer teaches us of the persons and relations within the Godhead.

The Father

Aside from the Article *Of Faith in the Holy Trinity*, Cranmer did not devote many words to defending the deity or personhood of the Father; he did not need to. However, his portrayal of the Father in the *BCP* is worth unpacking.

In common with all mainstream Church traditions and following Scriptural phraseology (for example, Matt 28:19–20), Cranmer teaches us that the Father is to be considered the first in order of the three divine persons. The Athanasian Creed (in common with the other Creeds) lays down this pattern: 'The Father is made of none: neither created nor begotten. The Son is of the Father alone: not made nor created, but begotten. The Holy Ghost is of the Father and of the Son neither made, nor created, nor begotten, but proceeding.'[1] In the *BCP*, the Father is almost always named first of the three, for, as Aquinas emphasised, the Father is the 'principle' of the Trinity.[2] Thus, in the

---

[1] 'The Athanasian Creed' is rather a misnomer: 'Ascribed to Athanasius, archbishop of Alexandria (c. 296–373), because of his reputation as a defender of orthodoxy, though it was originally composed in Latin, probably in Gaul during the first half of the sixth century, and possibly by Caesarius, who was bishop of Aries from 502 to 542.' Gerald Bray, ed., *Tudor Church Reform: The Henrician Canons of 1535 and the Reformatio Legum Ecclesiasticarum* (Woodbridge: Boydell, 2000), 174 fn 10.

[2] Letham, *Trinity*, 269. 'Principle' here means 'one from whom another proceeds,' conveying the same idea that the Father is not 'of' the Son or Spirit;

Confirmation, Wherein is Contained a Catechism for Children, the candidate(s) must recite the Apostles' Creed, after which the very first doctrinal question asks:

> *Question:* What doest thou chiefly learn in these articles of thy belief?

> *Answer:* First, I learn to believe in God the Father, who hath made me and all the world. Secondly, in God the Son who hath redeemed me and all mankind. Thirdly, in God the Holy Ghost, who sanctifieth me and all the elect people of God.[3]

It is to the Father then that the works of creation, salvation and judgement are properly ascribed. Consider the General Confession from The Order for the Administration of the Lord's Supper, or Holy Communion:

> Almighty God, Father of our Lord Jesus Christ, maker of all things, judge of all men, we knowledge and bewail our manifold sins and wickedness, which we from time to time most grievously have committed, by thought, word and deed, against thy divine Majesty: provoking most justly thy wrath and indignation against us: we do earnestly repent, and be heartily sorry for these our misdoings: the remembrance of them is grievous unto us, the burthen of them is intolerable: have mercy upon

---

he proceeds from neither. Rather, he is the one from whom they proceed. The Church Fathers would have been in agreement: Gregory of Nazianzus, for example, affirmed the 'monarchy' of the Father (Letham, *Trinity*, 168–69). To complete the picture, the same was true of the Reformers. Calvin also spoke repeatedly in this way, as Letham summarises: 'In all of God's works, the three work together... and in these activities there is this clear order. Behind this lies a relational order. The Father is first, from him is the Son, and from both is the Spirit' (Letham, *Trinity*, 302). See also Letham's discussion in Robert Letham, *The Holy Spirit* (Phillipsburg, NJ: P&R, 2023), 61-74.

[3] It is striking that the Trinity comes first here, before the recitation of the 10 Commandments or anything else. Also notable is the instruction at the very end: 'there shall none be admitted to the Holy Communion, until such time as he can say the Catechism, and be confirmed.' So Cranmer would not allow anyone to partake of the Lord's Supper until he or she could articulate the church's teaching on the Trinity! The *BCP* does not specify an age, merely 'when children come to the years of discretion.' On the Trinity and the Supper, see below.

us, have mercy upon us, most merciful Father, for thy Son our Lord Jesus Christ's sake: forgive us all that is past, and grant that we may ever hereafter serve and please thee, in newness of life, to the honour and glory of thy name: through Jesus Christ our Lord.

Notice here that it is the Father whom we address, it is the Father who is creator and judge, it is the Father against whom we have sinned and whose wrath we have provoked, it is the Father whose forgiveness we entreat, and it is the Father who will show us mercy and will grant transformation.[4]

This is not to say, of course, that the Son and Spirit have no part in these things: the prayer is uttered *through* Christ, who is named as our Lord. But the works are rightly attributed first to the Father: they are *his* works. This may surprise those who are more used to thinking, for example, of Christ as our judge (on which, see below). But Cranmer is entirely in line with Scripture here: Paul tells the Athenians that God 'has fixed a day on which he will judge the world in righteousness by a man whom he has appointed; and of this he has given assurance to all by raising him from the dead' (Acts 17:31).

This leads us to consider *how* the Father achieves his works – by what means? Cranmer would agree with Athanasius here: 'the Father does all things through the Word and in the Holy Spirit.'[5] It is the Father 'which of thy tender mercy didst give thine only Son Jesus Christ, to suffer death upon the cross for our redemption...'[6] It is the Father whom 'we beseech thee, leave us not comfortless; but send to us thine Holy Ghost to comfort us, and exalt us unto the same place whither our saviour Christ is gone before...'[7] It is the Father who gives the Son and sends the Spirit in order to achieve his works. Cranmer was extremely precise about this: never does his liturgy have us speaking of the Son sending the Father, nor of the Spirit working through the Father (or the Son). The Father is truly the fountainhead of the Trinity and of

---

[4] See too Christ's instruction to pray: 'Father... forgive us our sins...' (Luke 11:4).
[5] *Letter to Serapion* 1.28, quoted in Khaled Anatolios, *Retrieving Nicaea: The Development and Meaning of Trinitarian Doctrine* (Grand Rapids: Baker, 2011), 144.
[6] From The Order for Administration of Holy Communion.
[7] From the Collect for The Sunday after the Ascension Day. Once again, we hear Scripture in the background of these prayers: for instance, John 14:15–17 and Galatians 4:4–6.

the works of God. And yet he comes to us in and by the Son and the Spirit, by and in whom in turn we come to him. Therefore, it is to the Father that prayer is commonly uttered: the vast majority of Cranmer's prayers are addressed to the Father, through the Son. (As we will see, there are occasional pleas to the Son or Spirit when their particular properties or actions are in view.)

One particular aspect of the Father's character seems to have been particularly important to Cranmer. To what sort of a Father do we pray? The attribute that Cranmer regularly highlights is his mercy. As quoted above, he is the 'most merciful Father' who gave his Son 'of thy tender mercy.' The Litany reminds that he is God, the 'merciful Father, that despisest not the sighing of a contrite heart.' We may confess our sins with confidence 'that we may obtain forgiveness of the same by his infinite goodness and mercy.'[8] Many more examples could be given, for indeed, the Father's 'property is always to have mercy.'[9] Cranmer's Father is most certainly Almighty (another regular appellation in the *BCP*) and to be approached with a humble reverence appropriate to his holiness. However, he is not cold, remote, or harsh towards his people. He is a tenderly loving Father, ever ready to show mercy, to forgive sins and to bless those who ask through Christ.[10] This was a common theme among the Reformers. Luther prayed: 'Now through your mercy

---

[8] From the minister's invitation to confession in The Order for Morning Prayer. According to Brightman, *The English Rite*, 1:131, this was an entirely new 1552 addition to the *BCP*.

[9] From the Prayer of Humble Access in The Order for Administration of Holy Communion. This prayer 'is an excellent example of Cranmer's method of composition... it begins with a phrase from a priest's private prayer found in two missals printed before 1548. The rest of the prayer reflects the range of Cranmer's reading: possible sources of its language include the Litany of St Basil, the Book of Daniel, the Gospels of St Mark and St John, the Hereford Missal, the Litany, St Thomas Aquinas, Florus of Lyons, and Paschasius Radbert. With the exception of the gospel references, none is so literally reproduced as to be definitely identifiable as a source; but each, filtered through Cranmer's retentive memory, may have contributed something to the general sense, and a word or two of the actual phrasing.' Cuming, *Anglican Liturgy*, 43. The word 'always' is important here. As Article I reminds us, God is perfect and does not change, and so we can be sure that he will not suddenly lose his merciful character, or swing erratically from one emotion to another.

[10] This is partly why Cranmer teaches us to address God using the informal pronoun 'thou' (along with thy, thine, etc). We may speak to the Father (and the Son) using intimate, familiar terms. One thinks of Paul's reminder that as sons of God in Christ, by the Spirit we pray 'Abba, Father' (Romans 8:15).

implant in our hearts a comforting trust in your fatherly love, and let us experience the sweet and pleasant savor of a childlike certainty that we may joyfully call you Father, knowing and loving you and calling on you in every trouble.'[11] Tyndale rejoiced that Christ 'obtained that God should love us first, and be our Father, and that a merciful Father, that will consider our infirmities and weakness.'[12] As Cranmer put it in the Collect for the Twelfth Sunday after Trinity:

> Almighty and everlasting God, which art always more ready to hear than we to pray, and art wont to give more than either we desire or deserve; pour down upon us the abundance of thy mercy; forgiving us those things whereof our conscience is afraid, and giving unto us that that our prayer dare not presume to ask, through Jesus Christ our Lord.[13]

Michael Jensen comments along similar lines in a recent book on Anglican worship:

> How is God to be addressed? How does the Reformation Anglican liturgy script calling on God for the people of God? The General Confession of the Communion service is an example: 'Almighty God, Father of our Lord Jesus Christ, Maker of all things, Judge of all men.' We should add just one further repeated theme: he is also the 'merciful Father.' The God of the prayer book is sovereign; he is worth praying to since he is almighty – transcendent and unsurpassable. On occasion he is also addressed as 'Eternal God.' But he is also the 'Father,' the name of God learned from the prayer of Jesus, which features so often in Cranmer's services. The fatherhood of God was a scriptural theme rediscovered in the Reformation. It was a distinctive

---

[11] From Luther's 'Personal Prayer Book', quoted in Mark Rogers, '"Deliver Us from the Evil One": Martin Luther on Prayer,' *Themelios* 34 (2009): 337.
[12] The quotation is from *A Pathway into Scripture* and is cited by Ralph Werrell, 'Little Known Facts About William Tyndale's Theology: The Work of the Holy Spirit and the Covenant with Man,' *Churchman* 122 (2008): 315. Compare the prayer in the Litany: 'We humbly beseech thee, O Father, mercifully to look upon our infirmities...'
[13] According to Brightman, *The English Rite*, 2:503, this prayer has its origin in the Gelasian Sacramentary, but it has been significantly adapted by Cranmer.

feature of John Calvin's theological vision... it had a particular significance within his system, as it did for Cranmer: Christians can address God as 'Father' because they are his children by adoption in Christ. They have, by the cross of Christ, been welcomed into the family of God.[14]

This, then, is the Father that Cranmer presents to us in the *BCP* for our worship: merciful and mighty.

The Son

Vast amounts could be said about Cranmer's doctrine of the Son of God, and we shall explore some aspects of the Son's work in further detail below. For now, we begin with Canon 3 of the *Reformatio Legum Ecclesiasticarum*, 'Of Christ and the Mysteries of our Redemption':

> Furthermore, it is to be believed that when the fulness of time was come, the Son, who is the Word of the Father, took on a human nature in the womb of the blessed virgin Mary, of the substance of her flesh, so that the two natures, divine and human, have been inseparably conjoined, fully and perfectly, in unity of person. Out of them there is one Christ, true God and true man, who truly suffered, was crucified, died and was buried, he descended into hell and on the third day he rose again, and by his blood he has reconciled the Father to us, offering himself to him as a sacrifice, not only for original guilt, but also for all the sins which people have added to that by their own will.[15]

---

[14] Michael P. Jensen, *Reformation Anglican Worship: Experiencing Grace, Expressing Gratitude*, vol. 4 of *The Reformation Anglicanism Essential Library*, ed. Ashley Null and John W. Yates III (Wheaton, IL.: Crossway, 2021), 147.
[15] In Bray, *Tudor Church Reform*, 173. This statement owes much to the Athanasian Creed. It is also very similar to Article II of the Forty-Two, 'Of the Word or Son of God, which was made Very Man: The Son, which is the Word of the Father, took man's nature in the womb of the Blessed Virgin, of her substance: so that the two whole and perfect natures, that is to say the Godhead and the manhood, were joined together in one Person, never to be divided, whereof is one Christ, very God and very Man, who truly suffered, was crucified, dead and buried, to reconcile his Father to us and to be a sacrifice for all sin of man, both original and actual.' In Bray, *Documents*, 285–86.

This statement is typical of the full-blooded Nicene and Chalcedonian Christology which Cranmer embedded throughout his writings.

Cranmer is unmistakably clear on the Son's eternal divinity: he is 'the Son, who *is* the Word of the Father' (emphasis added). The Son of God is a fully divine person, coequal with his Father. He is therefore worthy of equal glory - hence the common refrain, 'glory be to the Father, and to the Son'). He is worthy of equal worship, although it is notable that the *BCP* rarely speaks explicitly of worshipping the Son. Rather, we worship the Father through the Son, by the Spirit (John 4:23–24). Christ is also the divine judge: the Collect for The First Sunday in Advent (echoing the Nicene Creed) refers to the 'last day when he shall come again in his glorious majesty to judge both the quick and the dead.' As we saw above, there is no contradiction here with the role of the Father in judgement: the Father achieves his task of judging the world *by* his Son, so that they may both be rightly spoken of as judge. As a more modern Anglican publication puts it: 'The Father shows his paternal generosity in at least three respects: first, providing the Son with a people; secondly, giving the Son, after his resurrection and ascension, Lordship over all things for all time, and, thirdly, giving the Son authority to exercise judgement at his Second Coming.'[16]

Given his divine personhood, Cranmer also teaches us that we may pray to the Son, as the Litany demonstrates:

> Son of God: we beseech thee to hear us.
> O Lamb of God, that takest away the sins of the world,
> Grant us thy peace.
> O Lamb of God, that takest away the sins of the world,
> Have mercy upon us...
> From our enemies defend us, O Christ...
> Both now and ever vouchsafe to hear us, O Christ...

This Article was lightly revised in 1563 and 1571. Griffith Thomas, *Principles of Theology*, 33, states that this also has its basis in the Augsburg Confession.
[16] Nicholas Okoh, Vinay Samuel and Chris Sugden, eds., *Being Faithful: The Shape of Historic Anglicanism Today – A Commentary on the Jerusalem Declaration Supplemented by the Way, the Truth and the Life. Theological Resources for a Pilgrimage to a Global Anglican Future* (London: Latimer Trust, 2009), 105. The whole commentary is infused with classic Anglican Trinitarianism. See also the comments on the creeds, 34, and diversity and unity, 60–61.

Graciously hear us, O Christ, graciously hear us, O
Lord Christ.[17]

As we have seen, prayer is normally to the Father through the Son.
However, it is at times appropriate to pray directly to the Son, when his
particular person or work is in view.[18]

This was also true for Cranmer on a more intimate, personal level.
In a letter to Bullinger, he concluded: 'May the Lord Jesus guide and
defend you by his holy Spirit!'[19] And to Joan Wilkinson (to whom he
wrote from prison, advising her to flee the country to escape Marian
persecution): 'And the Lord send his Holy Spirit to lead and guide you,
wheresoever you go!'[20] Aside from giving a rather beautiful insight
into his understanding of the personal relationship with Christ that
believers enjoy, and into his own pastoral concern, we also see once
again Cranmer's willingness to address the Son in petition. It is also
notable that Cranmer refers to 'his [Christ's] Holy Spirit' whom he may
send to guide his people.[21] The Son, then, is fully God, the eternal Word
of the Father, and to be worshipped as such.

Recent years have seen the emergence of a vigorous debate over the
relationship between Father and Son: where would Cranmer have
stood on issues such as whether the Son eternally submits (or even is
subordinate) to the Father?[22] The short answer is that we do not know
for certain, for he did not address these things directly. Indeed, Cranmer
does not speak often of Christ's obedience at all, and when he does, it
is clearly in reference to his incarnate obedience in going to the cross
(Phil 2:8). Even rarer are any mentions of submission.[23] Perhaps the

---

[17] See Brightman, *The English Rite*, 1:180–83 for some of the Latin sources for
these prayers.
[18] This fits with the pattern of Scripture, where we find occasional prayers to
Jesus (e.g., Acts 7:59–60, 1 Thess 3:11–13, Rev 22:20).
[19] Translation of the original Latin provided by Cox, *Works 2*, 431.
[20] Cox, *Works 2*, 445.
[21] Remember how Paul refers to the 'Spirit of Christ' in Romans 8:9; also see
Galatians 4:6.
[22] For an overview and reflections, see Letham, *Trinity*, 461–92.
[23] The *Sermon Concerning the Time of Rebellion* speaks of 'the strong and
perfect obedience whereby [Christ] submitted himself unto his Father, to be
obedient even unto the death of the cross' (Cox, *Works 2*, 192). This sermon
was something of a collaborative effort between Vermigli and Cranmer (Null,
Repentance, 227). It is possible that the language of submission is more
Vermigli's than Cranmer's, as Cranmer does not use it elsewhere. In any case,

closest we may get to an answer is in his inclusion of the *Te Deum* with its line: 'Thou art the king of glory, O Christ; Thou art the everlasting Son of the Father.'[24] Cranmer would gladly have us speak of the eternal Sonship of the Son: there is an everlasting Father–Son relationship, which entails some kind of eternal order (as we saw above, Cranmer was in agreement with historic orthodox theology on this). This is clearly an eternal order of mutual unity and love, which is accurately – though not fully – made known to us in the revealed (Scriptural) Trinity. Letham summarises Aquinas on this point: 'Although we attribute something of authority to the Father by his being principle, "we do not attribute any kind of subjection or inferiority to the Son, or to the Holy Ghost, to avoid any occasion of error" since the word *principle* "does not signify priority but origin."'[25] Cranmer would surely agree here. Beyond this, we cannot really go.

Before moving to Cranmer's theology of the Spirit, I will briefly note two other features of Cranmer's theology of the Son. Firstly, his precision in using the title *Christ*. As Cranmer's Article II states: 'the two whole and perfect natures, that is to say the Godhead and the manhood, were joined together in one Person, never to be divided, whereof is one Christ, very God and very Man...' Cranmer makes it unmistakably clear that he holds to an eternally, fully divine and eternally, fully human Lord: *Christ* is a title properly applied to the God–Man, the incarnate Word.

Secondly, the Son's work in our salvation. It is the Son (not the Father or the Spirit) who 'truly suffered, was crucified, died and was buried,' it is he who 'by his blood has... reconciled the Father to us, offering himself to him as a sacrifice.'[26] This is the reason why we approach the Father through the Son. It is he who, as the Litany says, is our 'only mediator and advocate.' It is he who is the Saviour (one of the most common ways in which the *BCP* refers to Christ). It is into him that we are ingrafted, as the Collect for All Saints Day reminds us: 'Almighty God,

---

the focus is still clearly on Christ's human submission, seen most clearly at the cross.

[24] The *Te Deum* is traditionally attributed to Ambrose of Milan. Notice again the direct address to God the Son.

[25] Letham, *Trinity*, 269. The quoted words here are from *Summa Theologica* 1.33.1.

[26] Cranmer regularly attaches the word 'precious' when he speaks of Christ's blood (and, on occasion, body), for instance the Litany: 'spare thy people whom thou hast redeemed with thy most precious blood.' Believers today could do much worse than to follow this example.

which hast knit together thy elect in one Communion and fellowship, in the mystical body of thy Son Christ our Lord'. It is he who sustains us: 'our Saviour Christ is both the first beginner of our spiritual life, (who first begetteth us unto God his Father,) and also afterward he is our lively food and nourishment'.[27] And it is Christ who shall raise us at the last, in the famous words of *The Order for the Burial of the Dead*:

> ...we therefore commit [the deceased's] body to the ground, earth to earth, ashes to ashes, dust to dust, in sure and certain hope of resurrection to eternal life, through our Lord Jesus Christ, who shall change our vile body, that it may be like to his glorious body, according to the mighty working whereby he is able to subdue all things to himself.[28]

It will be clear that none of the above is particularly unusual, let alone controversial, in terms of orthodox theology. As we shall have regular cause to reflect upon, Cranmer's great achievement was to weave these truths of the Bible into the *BCP*, so that they would lodge themselves in the hearts and minds of English churchgoers.

The Holy Spirit

Cranmer's *Forty-Two Articles* did not include what is today Article V of the Thirty-Nine, *Of the Holy Ghost*, although there is no doubt that he would have given it his hearty approval, theologically speaking.[29]

---

[27] Cranmer made this remark in Book 1 of *An Answer unto a Crafty and Sophistical Cavillation Devised by Stephen Gardiner, Doctor of Law, Late Bishop of Winchester, Against the True and Godly Doctrine of the Most Holy Sacrament of the Body and Blood of our Saviour Jesus Christ*. In Cox, *Works 1*, 40. See below for more on the Supper.

[28] Brightman, *The English Rite*, 2:858, notes that some of this prayer has its origins in the Sarum rite: *terram terre, cinerem cineri, puluerem pulueri*. However, the Latin made no mention of the hope of resurrection through Christ, and interestingly the priest commended the departed's soul to God, not his or her body to the ground.

[29] 'The Holy Ghost, proceeding from the Father and the Son, is of one substance, majesty, and glory, with the Father and the Son, very and eternal God.' This was added in 1563, 'probably because it was felt that something needed to be said about the Holy Spirit in order to reflect the Trinitarian pattern of the creeds more exactly.' (Gerald Bray, *The Faith We Confess: An Exposition of the Thirty-Nine Articles* (London: Latimer Trust, 2009), 37; see also Griffith Thomas, *Principles of Theology*, 90.) The Forty-Two Articles did, however, contain an article of *Blasphemy against the Holy Ghost* (XVI), while

For once again, we see that Cranmer held to a fully historic, orthodox Trinitarian theology: the third person of the Godhead is truly and fully divine. Cranmer approvingly cites the Church Fathers on this point:

> Didymus [the Blind] in his book *de Spirit Sancto*, which St Jerome did translate, proveth, that the Holy Ghost is very God, because he is in many places at one time, which no creature can be... And forasmuch as the Holy Ghost is in many men at one time, therefore, saith he, the Holy Ghost must needs be God. The same affirmeth St Basil [of Caesarea], that... the Holy Ghost was at one time in Habakkuk, and in Daniel in Babylon, and with Jeremy [Jeremiah] in prison, and with Ezekiel in Chober; whereby he proveth that the Holy Ghost is God.[30]

Therefore, the Spirit, as the Nicene Creed says, 'with the Father and the Son together, is worshipped and glorified.' He reigns alongside the Father and Son in unity. While it is not common in the *BCP* for prayers to be uttered to the Spirit, Cranmer included the – very Trinitarian – old Latin hymn *Veni, Creator Spiritus* in *The Form of Ordering Priests*. This hymn petitions the Spirit: 'Come Holy Ghost, eternal God, proceeding from above, Both from the Father and the Son, the God of peace and love. Visit our minds, and into us, thy heavenly grace inspire; That in all truth and godliness, we may have true desire.' Again, we see that while prayer is normally addressed to the Father, through the Son, by or in the Spirit, Cranmer teaches us that it is appropriate to supplicate the Spirit when his particular person and work is in view.

The quotation from *Veni, Creator Spiritus* leads us to touch briefly on the issue of the Spirit's procession. Cranmer was essentially a thoroughly Western theologian, so it is natural that he included the Western version of the Nicene creed with its phrase: 'And I believe in the Holy Ghost, the Lord and giver of life, who proceedeth from the Father *and the Son*' (emphasis added).[31] Cranmer has this in common with

---

what is now (with minor alterations) Article XVI of the Thirty-Nine: *Of Sin after Baptism*, was Article XV: *Of Sin against the Holy Ghost*.

[30] This quotation is from Book 3 of Cranmer's *Answer* to Gardiner. In Cox, *Works 1*, 97.

[31] MacCulloch's observes: 'Cranmer certainly had Greek liturgical texts in his library, but their effect on his thinking seems to have been minimal: the prayer of St Chrysostom... was derived from a 1528 Latin translation, as a misreading

the other Reformers: it would have been most surprising – virtually unthinkable – for him not to have included the *filioque* clause.[32] Canon 2 of the *Reformatio Legum Ecclesiasticarum* gives further proof of this:

> All children of God who are born again by Jesus Christ, shall believe with a pure heart, a good conscience and an unfeigned faith, and they shall confess that there is one living and true God, eternal and incorporeal, impassible, of unlimited power, wisdom and goodness, the creator and preserver of all things, both visible and invisible, and that in the unity of that divine nature there are three persons, of the same essence and eternity, the Father, the Son and the Holy Spirit, and that the Father is of himself, neither begotten of anyone else nor proceeding, and that the Son is begotten of the Father, and that the Holy Spirit proceeds from the Father and the Son, and that no diversity or inequality is to be understood in this distinction of persons, but that according to the divine substance, or (as they say) essence, they share everything alike and equally.[33]

This canon is very similar to Article I, *Of Faith in the Holy Trinity*; but notice the insistence on the double procession of the Spirit. 'There is no question that the divines of the formative period in Anglicanism defended the *Filioque*. They believed it to be the teaching of Scripture.'[34]

---

of the Greek in both Latin and English (*Cranmer*, 415–16).' However, for Cranmer's use of Chrysostom in his Eucharistic theology, see below.

[32] 'Filioque' is Latin for 'and the Son.' The *filioque* clause was added to the Nicene Creed by the Western churches from the sixth century onwards, in order to uphold the full deity of the Son and the identity of essence of the Father and the Son. However, to the Eastern churches, the *filioque* confused the distinct persons of the Father and the Son, and implied two separate sources for the Holy Spirit. (This summary is based on Letham, *Holy Spirit*, 51–58. Letham argues that there is in fact a great deal more theological agreement between East and West than might appear, and that, when each side understands which particular Trinitarian truths the other is seeking to maintain, there can be substantial harmony. Letham also suggests that Cyril of Alexandria's formulation *'from the Father in the Son'* would be satisfactory to both sides.)

[33] In Bray, *Tudor Church Reform*, 171–73. Bray notes that 'the classical Western position was not challenged by the Protestant reformers' (171 fn 3).

[34] William Craig, 'Does Omitting the *Filioque* Clause Betray Traditional Anglican Thought?' *ATR* 78 (1996): 425, and see the discussion 425–31. This

Part of the defence for the *filioque* is the insistence that the revealed (Economic) Trinity must truly reveal the realities of the eternal (Immanent) Trinity: the Scriptures certainly speak of the Spirit being sent by both the Father and the Son. It is no surprise then, that with Cranmer we find pleas to both the Son (for example, in the letters quoted above) and to the Father for the sending or granting of the Spirit (for instance, the Collect for *Quinquagesima*: 'O Lord... send thy Holy Ghost, and pour into our hearts that most excellent gift of charity... Grant this for thy only Son, Jesus Christ's sake.').

With the *filioque*, Cranmer is following in the footsteps of Augustine and Aquinas. It has been noted that part of Augustine's legacy is a tendency in the Western church towards modalism – the blurring or confusing of the three persons – and in particular to a loss of clarity over the divine personhood of the Spirit (even if these things are in fact a misreading of Augustine himself).[35] However, we may confidently clear Cranmer of such a tendency: his is a precisely articulated theology of a distinct, divine person.

What of the Spirit's particular work? For Cranmer, the Spirit is the one who applies God's salvific work to God's people. Once again, this is entirely in agreement with historical orthodoxy. Christopher Beeley summarises Gregory of Nazianzus: 'As the presence of God in the Christian life and the immediate cause of the knowledge of God in Christ, the Spirit is the means by which the Church, both corporately and as individual believers, comes to share in Christ's saving work.'[36] Or as Cranmer put it in the *Homily on Faith*: 'the Holy Ghost doth teach us to trust in God, and to call upon him as our Father.'[37] Calvin

---

was challenged – in Anglican circles – only later. See below.
[35] See Letham, *Trinity*, xxx, 209–28. Similar things can be said of Aquinas: Letham, *Trinity*, 272–75.
[36] Christopher A. Beeley, *Gregory of Nazianzus on the Trinity and the Knowledge of God: In Your Light We Shall See Light* (Oxford: Oxford University Press, 2008), 178. (Gregory was also a passionate defender of the Spirit's full divinity.)
[37] In Cox, *Works 2*, 138. The full title of the Homily is *A Short Declaration of the True, Lively and Christian Faith*. Cranmer quotes Augustine with approval in the preceding sentence. For an overview of the Homilies, and Cranmer's use of the Fathers in them, see MacCulloch, *Cranmer*, 372–76, and Null, *Repentance*, 213–31.

agreed, teaching that 'it is Christ who communicates to us his life "by the power of His Spirit."'[38]

Once again this is embedded in Cranmer's liturgy. In *The Ministration of Baptism to be used in the Church,* the minister prays:[39]

> We beseech thee for thy infinite mercies, that thou wilt mercifully look upon these children, sanctify them and wash them with thy Holy Ghost, that they, being delivered from thy wrath, may be received into the Ark of Christ's Church, and being steadfast in faith, joyful through hope, and rooted in charity, may so pass the waves of this troublesome world, that finally they may come to the land of everlasting life, there to reign with thee, world without end, through Jesus Christ our Lord. Amen.[40]

Here, it is the Spirit who (it is prayed) will so unite Christ's people with him that they will pass safely through this world and come to reign with him. On another occasion, the minister prays: 'that we may shew ourselves thankful... and that we may daily increase and go forwards, in the knowledge and faith of thee, and thy Son, by the Holy Spirit.' It is through the Holy Spirit that God 'has appointed diverse orders of Ministers in thy church.'[41] In the Collect for Purity quoted earlier, it is 'by the inspiration of thy Holy Spirit' that the Father will 'cleanse the thoughts of our hearts,' and, in the Collect for Good Friday, it is by the 'Spirit [that] the whole body of the Church is governed and sanctified.' This helps to explain Cranmer's retention of the plea at Morning Prayer (echoing Psalm 51:11): 'take not thy Holy Spirit from us'; for without the Spirit, we are dead. Cranmer is teaching believers to earnestly long for the Spirit's vivifying work in our lives.

We could give many further examples. However, we conclude this section with a striking example of Cranmer's understanding of – and confidence in – the Spirit's work. In September 1555, he wrote to Martyn and Story, two of the men charged with his interrogation on behalf of Queen Mary, part of the process that would shortly lead to

---

[38] Letham, *Trinity,* 306 (the quoted words are from Calvin's commentary on John 17:21).

[39] Interestingly, the 1552 *BCP* contained no *Order of Baptism for those of Riper Years.* This was added for the 1662 *BCP.*

[40] Brightman, *The English Rite,* 2:993, notes that this prayer has a Latin ancestor.

[41] These are both from *The Form of Ordering Priests.*

his condemnation and execution. Nevertheless, Cranmer finished his letter: 'God send you his Spirit to induce you into all truth!'[42]

Three Persons and One God

> O God, the Father of heaven: have mercy upon us miserable sinners... O God the Son, redeemer of the world: have mercy upon us miserable sinners... O God the Holy Ghost, proceeding from the Father and the Son: have mercy upon us miserable sinners... O holy, blessed and glorious Trinity, three persons and one God: have mercy upon us miserable sinners.

Thus begins the Litany; it is an excellent example of Cranmer's carefully constructed, precisely expressed Trinitarian liturgy. Cuming explains how Cranmer made use of a number of different sources, including earlier Latin litanies, to arrive at these opening sentences. He is worth quoting at length here:

> The Latin runs: *Pater de coelis Deus: miserere nobis. Fili redemptor mundi Deus: miserere nobis. Spiritus Sancte Deus: miserere nobis. Sancta Trinitas, unus Deus: miserere nobis...* with the addresses to the Persons of the Trinity [Cranmer] begins by translating literally; then, observing that the Holy Spirit is not given any attribute, he borrows a phrase from the Nicene Creed: *qui a Patre Filioque procedit.* The address to the Trinity is expanded on the lines of the next phrase but one in the *Commendatio: Qui es trines et unus Deus* ('Who art God, threefold and one'). But the word 'persons' recalls the Athanasian Creed, and the words 'blessed and glorious' come from the antiphon sung with that creed in Trinity week, *O beata et benedicta et glorious Trinitas.* An analysis of almost any part of Cranmer's liturgical work will yield results similar to these.[43]

By such skilful weaving together of sources, Cranmer presents us with a carefully nuanced Trinitarian theology. He successfully avoids tritheism: here is not three gods, but one God in three persons. And yet each person is addressed as God. This fits well with Article I, where the

---

[42] In Cox, *Works* 2, 447. For Martyn and Story, see MacCulloch, *Cranmer*, 573–81.
[43] Cuming, *Anglican Liturgy*, 36.

description 'without body, parts or passions, of infinite power, wisdom and goodness, the maker and preserver of all things both visible and invisible' is deliberately applied to the 'one living and true God' *before* the statement that 'in Unity of this Godhead there be three persons' (who then, it is stressed, are 'of one substance, power and eternity'!). This makes clear that all the attributes of God apply to all three divine persons. There is no danger, though, of the drift towards modalism inherited from Augustine and Aquinas: each person is addressed in terms particular to them. Furthermore, each person, as fully divine, is called upon for mercy; yet it is not three gods who show mercy, but again one God in three persons, distinct and yet indivisible. Gregory of Nazianzus' statement that famously delighted John Calvin is apt here: 'No sooner do I conceive of the one than I am illuminated by the splendour of the three; no sooner do I distinguish them than I am carried back to the one.'[44] It is not too much of a stretch to imagine that it delighted Cranmer too.

Letham observes, 'In the West... philosophers of religion who are also Christian customarily refer to a generic "God" all the time, the Trinity going without a mention.'[45] This is partly because of the Western tendency to begin with the essence of God rather than the persons, in contrast to 'the Greek Fathers [who] begin with the persons rather than the common nature.'[46] In addition to a blurring of the persons into an indistinct entity called 'God', this can also (perhaps even worse) 'leave the impression that there is... some fourth thing called "God" beside the Father, Son and Spirit.'[47] Once again, however, we may clear Cranmer of such charges. Indeed, Cranmer not infrequently starts with the persons (as above in the Litany) – or is at least very quick to distinguish them. But nor would Cranmer have us veer anywhere near tritheistic (or subordinationist) territory. He was even so bold as to to remind Henry VIII of his Trinitarian essentials: 'It is not the use of scripture to attribute to one person of the Trinity peculiarly that thing which doth express the three persons in one deity. And we must not repute for God only Jesus Christ, but also the Father and the Holy Ghost.'[48]

[44] From his *Oration on Holy Baptism* 40. Quoted in Letham, *Trinity*, 175.
[45] Letham, *Trinity*, 496. See also xxxii–xxxiii.
[46] Anatolios, *Retrieving Nicaea*, 231.
[47] Michael Reeves, *The Good God: Enjoying Father, Son and Spirit* (Milton Keynes: Paternoster, 2012), 16. Reeves makes this remark in reference to the 'Trinity Shield' illustration.
[48] Cranmer made this comment in the *Corrections of The Institution of a Christian Man, by Henry VIII. With Archbishop Cranmer's Annotations* (in Cox,

Such a carefully articulated doctrine of the triune God is surely a very deep need among believers today; we shall reflect on this further below. We now turn to consider how Cranmer's doctrine of the Trinity applied to certain areas of Christian belief and practice.

Salvation and Worship

As we have already noted, salvation is a Trinitarian work. The Creeds remind us that all three persons of the Trinity enact the work of salvation in unity.[49]

Ashley Null makes it clear that Cranmer held to the Reformed stance on predestination (as shown in the famous response at Morning Prayer: 'make thy chosen people joyful'), which is a Trinitarian work – although not one that absolves human beings of their own moral responsibility: 'A Christian believed in the Lord by his own will and free choice. Nevertheless, salvation was not determined by human consent because the gift of grace imparted the Holy Spirit which brought about whatever good pertained to salvation, including consent.'[50] The same is true of what we might call justification and sanctification: 'God pardoned a sinner based on the extrinsic righteousness of Christ which the believer laid hold of through the divine gift of faith. At the same time, however, the Holy Spirit indwelt the believer and reordered his desires by shedding an intrinsic love into his heart.'[51] Perhaps the best summary of Cranmer's understanding of Trinitarian salvation comes from his commentary on Matthew 3, quoted by Null:

> In his own hand, Cranmer described the justification, sanctification and eternal salvation of the elect wholly in terms of divine activity. The elect were 'those given to the [Son] by the Father' whom 'the Son of God liberates from the power of Satan, purges, sanctifies, protects

Works 2, 100). For the background to the 'Bishop's Book' – as *The Institution of a Christian Man* became known – see, for example, Null, *Repentance*, 121.

[49] On this, Cranmer would have agreed with his great opponent Gardiner, who wrote: 'Our Saviour Christ, by the decree of the whole Trinity, took man's nature upon him, to suffer death for our redemption.' Cox, *Works 1*, 82.

[50] Null, *Repentance*, 202.

[51] Null, *Repentance*, 211. The last phrase in this sentence shows Cranmer's debt to Augustine. Null explores this in detail, 157–71.

and leads to him through his Holy Spirit until the day in which he will hand this kingdom to God the Father.'[52]

This Trinitarian salvific work (and man's responsibility to respond in faith) is stamped all over the *BCP*. For example, here is the absolution from Morning Prayer:

> Almighty God, the Father of our Lord Jesus Christ, which desireth not the death of a sinner, but rather that he may turn from his wickedness and live... pardoneth and absolveth all them which truly repent, and unfeignedly believe his holy Gospel. Wherefore we beseech him to grant us true repentance and his Holy Spirit, that those things may please him, which we do at this present, and that the rest of our life hereafter may be pure and holy: so that at the last we may come to his eternal joy, through Jesus Christ our Lord.[53]

It is no surprise, therefore, that the first and immediate human response to such a salvation is to praise and glorify the triune God. The doxology, 'Glory be to the Father, and to the Son, and to the Holy Ghost...' follows virtually every remembrance and rehearsal of salvation in the *BCP*.

This leads us to the Trinitarian nature of human worship in Cranmer's thought. The Trinity is the central, essential framework of worship: Anglican worship is Trinitarian worship. Anything else is not Anglican worship at all (nor indeed Christian worship at all!). Worship is a response to, and a participation in, Father, Son and Spirit. Cranmer once again would agree with Gregory of Nazianzus, whose 'single definition of piety' is 'the worship of the Father and Son and Holy Spirit, the one Divinity and power in the three.'[54] Cranmer applied this principle to all aspects of corporate Christian worship, as we can see in the following examples.

Prayer is perhaps the ultimate expression of Christian worship, and the fact '[t]hat Cranmer called his book the Book of Common Prayer and

---

[52] Null, *Repentance,* 225 (punctuation original). This represents Cranmer's mature, fully Reformed view of salvation. See also Article XVII of the Forty-Two (also XVII of the Thirty-Nine), *Of Predestination and Election,* in Bray, *Documents,* 294–95.

[53] Brightman, *The English Rite,* 1:131–33, notes that this absolution was entirely new for the 1552 *BCP*.

[54] *Oration* 22.12, quoted in Beeley, *Gregory of Nazianzus on the Trinity,* 188.

not the Book of Common Worship should not escape our notice. The very structure of the prayers written for the prayer book... frames the congregation in its relationship to God.'.[55] As Letham comments, 'Prayer is, *inter alia,* an exploration of the Holy Trinity.'[56] Cranmer would agree: there is no prayer in the *BCP* that does not have a Trinitarian framework. We have seen this already, so here we may briefly demonstrate that this is true of differing forms of prayer.[57] Thus, in the exhortation at Holy Communion, we are urged to offer thanksgiving:

> And above all things, ye must give most humble and hearty thanks to God the Father, the Son, and the Holy Ghost, for the redemption of the world by the death and passion of our Saviour Christ...

At Morning Prayer, the minister instructs the congregation to ask for the Father's forgiveness and provision:

> ...the scripture moveth us in sundry places, to acknowledge and confess our manifold sins and wickedness, and that we should not dissemble nor cloak them before the face of Almighty God our heavenly Father, but confess them... and to ask those things which be requisite and necessary, as well for the body as the soul.

These petitions will be granted, not because of our own merits, but because of God's gracious promise in Christ:

> Spare thou them, O God, which confess their faults. Restore thou them that be penitent, according to thy promises declared unto mankind, in Christ Jesu our Lord. And grant, O most merciful father, for his sake, that we may hereafter live a godly, righteous, and sober life, to the glory of thy holy name. Amen.

And while prayer in or by the Spirit is not a particularly dominant note in the *BCP*, Cranmer included the lines of the *Veni, Creator Spiritus,* addressed to the Spirit: 'According to thy promise made, thou givest speech of grace; That through thy help, the praise of God, may sound

---

55 Jensen, *Reformation Anglican Worship*, 21.
56 Letham, *Trinity*, 509.
57 'Prayer' here in the broader common sense of 'addressing God' rather than the technical definition of 'requesting.'

in every place.' Augustine, perhaps belying his reputation, prayed with delight to each person of the Trinity:

> O Lord our God, we believe in you, Father and Son and Holy Spirit... And if you, God and Father, were yourself also the Son your Word Jesus Christ, were yourself also your gift of the Holy Spirit, we would not read in the documents of truth God sent his Son (Gal 4:4), nor would you, only-begotten one, have said of the Holy Spirit, whom the Father will send in my name (Jn 14:26), and, whom I will send you from the Father (Jn 15:26).[58]

For Cranmer too, prayer is a Trinitarian exercise.

The same applies to preaching.[59] At the end of *The Form of Consecrating of an Archbishop or Bishop,* the presiding minister prays: 'Most merciful Father, we beseech thee to send down upon this thy servant, thy heavenly blessing, and so endue him with thy Holy Spirit, that he preaching thy word...' In *The Form for Ordering Priests,* it is desired that the ordinand(s) 'will continually pray for the heavenly assistance of the Holy Ghost, from God the Father, by the mediation of our only mediator and saviour Jesus Christ, that by daily reading and weighing of the Scriptures, ye may wax riper and stronger in your ministry.'[60] In Book 3 of his *Answer* to Gardiner, Cranmer wrote: 'And I express St Cyprian's mind truly... when I say, that... the Spirit of God is said to be... in his word when it is sincerely preached, with the Holy Spirit working mightily in the hearts of the hearers.'[61] Preaching is thus the setting

---

[58] Augustine, *On the Trinity,* 15.28.51, *The Works of Saint Augustine: A Translation for the 21st Century: The Trinity,* ed. John. E. Rotelle, trans. Edmund Hill, 2d ed. (Hyde Park, NY: New City Press, 2015), 443.

[59] See Jensen, *Reformation Anglican Worship,* 75–106, for an exploration of the Reformed Anglican doctrine and practice of preaching. Cranmer's dear friend Hugh Latimer is generally acknowledged to have been the finest preacher of the English Reformation.

[60] Also: 'Receive the Holy Ghost... and be a faithful dispenser of the word of God, and of his holy Sacraments.'

[61] In Cox, *Works 1,* 180–81. The full quotation is interesting for several reasons: 'And I express St Cyprian's mind truly, and not a whit discrepant from my doctrine here, when I say, that the divinity may be said to be poured, or put sacramentally into the bread; as the Spirit of God is said to be in the water of baptism, when it is truly ministered, or in his word when it is sincerely preached, with the Holy Spirit working mightily in the hearts of the hearers.' A

forth of the word of Christ, by the power of the Spirit, with the blessing of the Father. Even if he articulates this less fully, Cranmer here is in agreement with Calvin and the other Reformers.[62]

We may briefly also mention singing: Cranmer clearly approved of sung worship, as his inclusion of canticles and hymns, all of which are solidly Trinitarian, proves. Singing is a further way for believers to delight in the Trinity.[63]

We have not touched here on works of God such as creation and provision – there are many prayers for provision in the *BCP* – but we would find the same Trinitarian patterns there.[64] The same is true of what may be more broadly termed worship (in the sense of a whole life offered to God, Romans 12:1–2), for instance, mission or marriage.[65] For Cranmer, the Trinity shapes all things.

We now shall explore two further areas in greater detail: the word and the sacrament, for, as Ashley Null and John W. Yates III put it: 'Here is the heart of Cranmer's liturgical vision: divine gracious love, constantly communicated by the Holy Spirit in the regular repetition

---

further striking insight into Cranmer's thinking on preaching is found in his letter written to preachers on behalf of Edward VI: 'it is not his majesty's mind hereby clearly to extinct the lively teaching of the word of God by sermons... as for the time the Holy Ghost shall put into the preacher's mind, but that rash, contentious, hot, and undiscreet preachers should be stopped...' (in Cox, *Works 2*, 512). Clearly Cranmer did not wish to quench the Spirit; but neither did he want completely unregulated preaching, however spiritual it may claim to be.

[62] For Calvin, see, for example, Michael Reeves, 'The Trinity and Preaching,' in *The Essential Trinity: New Testament Foundations and Practices*, ed. Brandon D. Crowe and Carl R. Trueman (London: Apollos, 2016), 257–73.

[63] See Jensen, *Reformation Anglican Worship*, 157–71, for an overview of sung worship during the English Reformation.

[64] We see the connection between creation and salvation in Cranmer's comment: 'And as Almighty God by his most mighty word and his holy Spirit and infinite power brought forth all creatures in the beginning and ever sithens [since] hath preserved them... even so by the same word and power he worketh in us, from time to time, this marvellous spiritual generation and wonderful spiritual nourishment and feeding, which is wrought only by God, and is comprehended and received of us by faith.' From Book 3 of his *Answer to Gardiner*, in Cox, *Works 1*, 198.

[65] Note the benediction for the couple in *The Form of the Solemnisation of Matrimony*: 'God the Father, God the Son, God the Holy Ghost, bless, preserve and keep you...'

of Scripture's promises through Word and sacrament, inspires grateful human love, drawing believers toward God, their fellow human beings, and the lifelong pursuit of godliness.'[66]

The Scriptures

Much has been written about Cranmer and the Bible. Here we consider this area from a Trinitarian angle. Ashley Null has conducted a 'reappraisal of Cranmer's understanding of scripture... by taking a direct look at his "Great Commonplaces."'[67] In these notes, Thomas Cranmer stated his fundamental approach to the Bible: 'Scripture comes not from the church, but from God and has authority by the Holy Spirit.'[68] This 'very pure word of God' – as the *BCP* Preface puts it – is a self-revelatory gift from the Holy Trinity to mankind, so that we may come to know God:

> Cranmer believed that God had given his divine authority to the Bible because it was his personal instrument to bring salvation to the world. Augustine, Cranmer's favorite patristic theologian, had said as much in his *Confessions*: 'By no means would God have given such eminent authority to the Scriptures throughout all the earth, unless he had wanted people both to believe in him and seek him through this means.'[69]

We may be even more specific: the Bible is the Father's witness to Son, by the Spirit. For, as Cranmer's *Homily on Scripture* tells us, 'In those books we shall find the Father, from whom, the Son, by whom, and the Holy Ghost, in whom, all things have their being and keeping up;

---

[66] Ashley Null and John W. Yates III, 'A Manifesto for Reformation Anglicanism,' in *Reformation Anglicanism: A Vision for Today's Global Communion*, vol. 1 of *The Reformation Anglicanism Essential Library*; ed. Ashley Null and John W. Yates III; (Wheaton, IL.: Crossway, 2017), 199–200.

[67] Ashley Null, 'Thomas Cranmer and the Anglican Way of Reading Scripture,' *Anglican and Episcopal History* 75 (2006): 493.

[68] Null, 'Cranmer and the Anglican Way'. The reference to Scripture not proceeding from the church comes in the context of debate with the Roman Catholic view, as Null shows. The Scriptures' provenance means that they are the ultimate authority, by which all creeds, councils and church authorities must be judged, as, for example, Articles VII, XXII and XXIII of the Forty-Two (VIII, XXI and XXII of the Thirty-Nine) make clear: see Bray, *Documents*, 289, 297.

[69] Null, 'Cranmer and the Anglican Way', 494.

and these three Persons to be but one God and one substance.'[70] Let us unpack this statement in a little more detail.

Firstly, the Scriptures are a gift from the Father. As the Homily says: 'Let us thank God heartily for this his great and special gift, beneficial favour, and fatherly providence. Let us be glad to revive this precious gift of our Heavenly Father.'[71]

Secondly, the Scriptures' principal subject is the person and work of the Son, the Word become flesh. The Old and New Testaments are 'the books of Christ's gospel and doctrine.'[72]

Thirdly, the Scriptures are inspired by the Holy Spirit: Cranmer believed:

> ...that the role of the Holy Spirit was to point to Christ and his work... In the case of the writers of the New Testament, the Holy Spirit had the special task of so inspiring their remembrances and research that they were able perfectly to pass on to future generations the essentials of salvation that Christ had revealed.[73]

But how can one understand these Scriptures correctly, since they contain such mysteries? Cranmer anticipated this very question in his Preface to the Great Bible: what 'if we understand not that we read that is contained in the books?'[74] Here too, the answer is Trinitarian. For the Spirit of God, who inspired the Scriptures and taught the first disciples, does not change, as the Collect for Whitsunday reminds us:

---

[70] The full title is *A Fruitful Exhortation to the Reading and Knowledge of Holy Scripture*. In John Griffiths, ed., *The Two Books of Homilies Appointed to be Read In Churches* (Oxford: Oxford University Press, 1859), 8. It is not hard to hear echoes of the Church Fathers here.

[71] In Griffiths, *Homilies*, 15. The language of 'reviving' is a reference to 2 Timothy 1:6: '...I remind you to fan into flame the gift of God...'

[72] Griffiths, *Homilies*, 11. See also Article VI of the Forty-Two (VII of the Thirty-Nine), in Bray, *Documents*, 288–89: 'both in the Old and New Testaments, everlasting life is offered to mankind by Christ.'

[73] Null, 'Reading Scripture,' 500.

[74] This was written for the second (1540) edition of the English Bible, sometimes called *Cranmer's Bible* (see MacCulloch, *Cranmer*, 258–60), quoted here in Cox, *Works 2*, 120. It is properly called *A Prologue or Preface Made by the Most Reverend Father in God, Thomas, Archbishop of Canterbury, Metropolitan and Primate of England*. Reading both the *Preface* and the *Homily on Scripture*, one is struck once again by Cranmer's indebtedness to the Fathers, especially Chrysostom and Gregory of Nazianzus.

God, which as upon this day hast taught the hearts of
thy faithful people, by the sending to them the light of
thy Holy Spirit; grant us by the same Spirit to have a
right judgement in all things, and evermore to rejoice
in his holy comfort; through the merits of Christ Jesus
our saviour; who liveth and reigneth with thee, in the
unity of the same Spirit, one God, world without end.

The same Spirit who breathed out the Scriptures to speak of Christ
will illumine the minds of God's people to understand and to believe
in him. Scriptures therefore are a gift to *all* God's people, 'For the Holy
Ghost hath so ordered and attempered the scriptures, that in them
as well publicans, fishers, and shepherds may find their edification,
as great doctors their erudition.'[75] This being so, all of God's people
should desire to increase in knowledge:

Go to thy curate and preacher; shew thyself to be
desirous to know and learn: and I doubt not but God,
seeing thy diligence and readiness (if no man else teach
thee,) will himself vouchsafe with his holy Spirit to
illuminate thee, and to open unto thee that which was
locked from thee.[76]

For, as the Homily says, 'Chrysostom saith, that "man's human and
worldly wisdom or science needeth not to the understanding of
Scripture, but the revelation of the Holy Ghost, who inspireth the
true meaning unto them that with humility and diligence do search
therefore."'[77] Not only, though, does the Spirit enable us to understand
the Scriptures. He also sanctifies us through them: Cranmer believed
that 'the Holy Spirit worked through the administration of God's word
as a divine instrument to bring about spiritual growth in a person's
life.'[78] Indeed, 'the books of the prophets and apostles, and all holy writ

---

[75] Preface to the Great Bible, in Cox, *Works* 2, 120–21.

[76] Preface to the Great Bible, in Cox, *Works* 2, 120–21. Note in this second
quotation Cranmer's usual careful balance: the Spirit is quite capable of
illuminating the eager mind without any human help. Nevertheless, it is
normal for God to use human teachers (the 'curate and preacher') for the
instruction of his people. It is worth remembering that Cranmer is writing
into a context where most Christians could neither read nor afford their own
personal Bible. I shall return to this point later on.

[77] In Griffiths, *Homilies*, 14.

[78] Null, 'Reading Scripture,' 512.

inspired by the Holy Ghost, [are] the instruments of our salvation.'[79] The Spirit, through the word, conforms believers to the image of Christ.

Once again, Cranmer is articulating Reformed theology. Tyndale wrote of the Scriptures:

> For as they came not by the will of man, so may they not be drawn or expounded after the will of man: but as they came by the Holy Ghost, so must they be expounded and understood by the Holy Ghost. The scripture is that wherewith God draweth us unto him .... The scriptures spring out of God and flow unto Christ, and were given to lead us to Christ.[80]

Given that the Great Bible was a revision and expansion of Tyndale's work, it is not too much to think that Cranmer's view of the Scriptures was influenced by the great translator. Cranmer would affirm along with Calvin that it is ultimately the Scriptures which contain all we need to know of God and of ourselves.[81]

There is one further aspect to dwell on here. For Cranmer, the Scriptures do not merely hold hope for this life. Rather, they are God's instrument, causing believers to persevere through this world to everlasting life in the presence of the triune God. In the closing prayer for Confirmation, Wherein is Contained a Catechism for Children, the minister prays:

> Almighty everliving God, which makest us both to will and to do those things that be good and acceptable unto thy Majesty... let thy fatherly hand we beseech thee ever be over them, let thy Holy Spirit ever be with them, and so lead them in the knowledge and obedience of thy word, that in the end they may obtain the everlasting life, through our Lord Jesus Christ...

Not only do believers, through God's word, come to find their eternal home in the triune God: the triune God makes his home in and with believers, forever (Rev 21:3). In the Homily, Cranmer writes: 'He that keepeth the words of Christ is promised the love and favour of God; and

---

[79] Preface, in Cox, *Works* 2, 120.
[80] The quotation is from *The Obedience of a Christian Man*, cited in Werrell, 'Little Known Facts About William Tyndale's Theology,' 315–16.
[81] Book 1 of the *Institutes*.

that he shall be the dwelling place or temple of the Blessed Trinity.'[82] This has a distinctly Augustinian flavour: it is 'the Holy Spirit of which [God] has given us that makes us abide in God and him in us.' The great early theologian eagerly looked forward to full contemplation of the Trinity: 'That one God, therefore, Father, Son and Holy Spirit, whose manifestation will mean nothing but joy which will not be taken away from the just (Jn 16:22; Lk 10:42), a joy to come for which someone sighs...'[83] As Null summarises: 'the Holy Spirit enabled [believers] to come to a personal saving faith through the witness of the New and Old Testaments so that believers might dwell in Christ and he in them.'[84]

No wonder, then, that Cranmer so desired an English translation of the Scriptures to be readily available for the people to 'read, mark, learn and inwardly digest,' as the Collect for The Second Sunday in Advent so famously puts it; nor that he was so delighted when Henry VIII finally gave his assent for such a Bible to be placed in every parish in England.[85] For if Christian people are to know and love their triune God, they must have his word.

Holy Communion

It would be a great mistake if we failed to consider the work of the Trinity in the Lord's Supper. Here we shall focus on Cranmer's mature Reformed theology of the 1550s, rather than tracing the development of his theology of the Supper, which has been well documented by others.[86] Null states that the Communion service is the 'ultimate expression of Cranmer's vision of God's gracious love inspiring human love' which 'he intended to be the central act of English worship.'[87] It is, of course, gloriously Trinitarian.

---

[82] In Griffiths, Homilies, 9. Note Null's comment: 'Since both testaments point to Christ, the "Homily on Scripture" could even use such phrases as the "words of Holy Scripture," "this Word of God" and "the Word of Christ" interchangeably.' Null, 'Reading Scripture,' 507.

[83] De Trinitate, 15.17.31; 1.13.31, trans. Hill.

[84] Null, 'Reading Scripture,' 500. See also Null's five marks of 'the historic Anglican way of reading the Bible,' 524–25.

[85] See MacCulloch, Cranmer, 196–97.

[86] Null, after surveying recent scholarship on Cranmer's theological development, agrees with MacCulloch that Cranmer was a 'committed protestant' by 1532: Null, Repentance, 16; see also 120–33.

[87] Null, Repentance, 26. This statement may raise some evangelical eyebrows. We will reflect further on the relationship between evangelicals and the Lord's

The Communion service is framed with Trinitarian prayers, beginning with the Collect for Purity (quoted above), and ending with 'the blessing of God Almighty, the Father, the Son, and the Holy Ghost, be amongst you and remain with you always. Amen.' The recitation of the Nicene Creed, the explanation of the Supper by the minister, and the further congregational prayers all reinforce this Trinitarian structure.[88]

The service reminds us that the Son is a gift to us from the Father:

> Dearly beloved, forasmuch as our duty is to render to Almighty God our Heavenly Father most hearty thanks, for that he hath given his Son our Saviour Jesus Christ, not only to die for us, but also to be our spiritual food and sustenance, as it is declared unto us, as well by God's word as by the holy Sacraments of his blessed body and blood...

It is the Father who graciously allows us to partake of his Son through the bread and wine:

> Hear us O merciful Father we beseech thee; and grant that we, receiving these thy creatures of bread and wine, according to thy Son our Saviour Jesus Christ's holy institution, in remembrance of his death and passion, may be partakers of his most blessed body and blood...[89]

And so it is the Father to whom – through the Son – we offer our own sacrifice:

> Lord and heavenly Father, we thy humble servants entirely desire thy fatherly goodness, mercifully to accept this our sacrifice of praise and thanksgiving... And here we offer and present unto thee, O Lord, our

Supper in the final chapter. See Brightman, *The English Rite*, 638–721, for the Latin sources, and the differences between 1549 and 1552.

[88] J. I. Packer has noted the 'sin-grace-faith' pattern in the Communion service (e.g., J. I. Packer, *The Gospel in the Prayer Book* (Abingdon: Marcham Manor Press, 1966), 6). It is perhaps not entirely coincidental that this is a threefold cycle.

[89] Also: 'Grant us therefore (gracious Lord) so to eat the flesh of thy dear Son Jesus Christ, and to drink his blood...'

selves, our souls, and bodies, to be a reasonable, holy, and lively sacrifice unto thee...[90]

Once again in the *BCP*, we encounter a gracious and merciful Father, who through the gift of his Son fills his people with his 'grace and heavenly benediction.'

Equal praise is due to the Son, as to the Father, at the Supper. For it is Christ (not the Father, nor the Spirit) who 'by his one oblation of himself once offered' on the cross made 'a full, perfect and sufficient sacrifice, oblation, and satisfaction, for the sins of the whole world.' It is Christ who 'did institute, and in his holy gospel command us to continue, a perpetual memory of that his precious death, until his coming again.' It is Christ who invites us to come to him with the 'comfortable words'. It is he who washes our souls with 'his most precious blood.' It is on Christ that we 'feed... in thy heart by faith with thanksgiving,' and, it is to Christ that we are united, as the minister prays, 'that we may evermore dwell in him, and he in us.'[91] The closing doxology mingles petition and praise to the Son:

> O Lord, the only begotten Son Jesu Christ: O Lord God, Lamb of God, Son of the Father, that takest away the sins of the world, have mercy upon us: Thou that takest away the sins of the world, have mercy upon us. Thou that takest away the sins of the world, receive our prayer. Thou that sittest at the right hand of God the Father, have mercy upon us: For thou only art holy, Thou only art the Lord. Thou only, (O Christ,) with the Holy Ghost, art most high in the glory of God the Father. Amen.

---

[90] Or: 'Almighty and everliving God, we most heartily thank thee, for that thou dost vouchsafe to feed us, which have duly received these holy mysteries, with the spiritual food of the most precious body and blood of thy Son our saviour Jesus Christ, and dost assure us thereby of thy favour and goodness toward us...'

[91] Note the similarities to the language used of Scripture. In Book 3 of his *Answer* to Gardiner, Cranmer made a striking comment linking the Lord's Supper to Christ's marriage to the church: citing Irenaeus, he says that at the Supper, we 'feed of Christ's very flesh, and drink his very blood. And we be in such sort united to him, that his flesh is made our flesh, and his holy Spirit uniting him and us so together, that we be flesh of his flesh, and bone of his bones, and make all one mystical body, whereof he is the head, and we the members.' In Cox, *Works 1*, 150.

How, though, do communicants 'eat the flesh of thy dear Son Jesus Christ, and... drink his blood'? For, as Cranmer wrote in his *Answer to Gardiner*:

> Of these words of St Augustine it is most clear, that the profession of the catholic faith is, that Christ (as concerning his bodily substance and nature of man) is in heaven, and not present here with us in earth. For the nature and property of a very body is to be in one place, and to occupy one place, and not to be everywhere, or in many places at one time.[92]

The Son has ascended bodily to his Father's right hand, and so it cannot be that the bread and wine are physically transformed into his body and blood.

The answer is the work of the Holy Spirit. The minister explains: 'if with a truly penitent heart and lively faith, we receive that holy Sacrament (for then we spiritually eat the flesh of Christ, and drink his blood, then we dwell in Christ and Christ in us, we be one with Christ, and Christ with us).' Packer comments, 'It is a pity that Cranmer nowhere worked out his insights into the Spirit's work.'[93] Perhaps this is true of the 1552 Communion service: it could do more to explain precisely how the Spirit is at work.[94] However, Reformed theology is clearly present, and Cranmer himself was not in the least unclear:

> How often do I teach and repeat again and again, that as corporally with our mouths we eat and drink the sacramental bread and wine, so spiritually with our

---

92 From Book 2, in Cox, *Works 1*, 95.

93 Packer, 'Cranmer's Catholic Theology,' 262.

94 Although we should note that Cranmer actually removed a reference to the Holy Spirit in deference to Bucer. In the 1549 *BCP* the minister asks that the Father 'with thy Holy Spirit and Word vouchsafe to bless and sanctify these thy gifts and creatures of bread and wine, so that they may be unto us the body and blood of thy most dearly beloved Son Jesus Christ.' Cranmer revised this for the 1552 *BCP*, Bucer being concerned that the words might imply a 'change in the eucharistic elements' (MacCulloch, *Cranmer*, 416). The limited references to the Spirit in the Communion service were perhaps then deliberate in order to avoid confusion. (Interestingly, this earlier version of the prayer has reappeared in a slightly modified form in more recent prayer books – for example, *The Alternative Service Book* and *Common Worship* – and has become quite well known.)

hearts, by faith, do we eat Christ's very flesh, and drink his very blood, and do both feed and live spiritually by him, although corporally he be absent from us, and sitteth in heaven at his Father's right hand![95]

Christ, then, is really, *spiritually*, present at the Supper – that is, really present by his Spirit. Indeed, at the Supper, the Spirit lifts us up by faith to the heavens to be nourished as we feed on Christ.[96] In a remarkable passage, citing Chrysostom, Cranmer writes:

[I]n our minds by faith we ascend up into heaven, to eat him [Christ] there, although sacramentally, as in a sign and figure, he be in the bread and wine... He [Chrysostom] saith also in many places that 'We ascend into heaven, and do eat Christ sitting there above.' And where St Chrysostom and other authors do speak of the wonderful operation of God in his sacraments, passing all man's wit, senses and reason, they meant not of the working of God in the water, bread, and wine, but of the marvellous working of God in the hearts of them that receive the sacraments; secretly, inwardly, and spiritually transforming them, renewing, feeding, comforting and nourishing them with his flesh and blood, through his most holy Spirit, the same flesh and blood still remaining in heaven.[97]

And again, drawing on Augustine:

For as Christ is a spiritual meat, so is he spiritually eaten and digested with the spiritual part of us, and giveth us spiritual and eternal life, and is not eaten, swallowed, and digested with our teeth, tongues, throats and bellies... And according unto the same, St Augustine saith: 'Prepare not thy jaws, but thy heart...'

[95] This quotation is from *The Answer of Thomas, Archbishop of Canterbury &c., Against the False Calumniations of Doctor Richard Smith, Who Hath Taken Upon Him To Confute The Defence Of The True and Catholic Doctrine Of The Body and Blood Of Our Saviour Christ* in Cox, *Works 1*, 373. For the background to this, see MacCulloch, *Cranmer*, 487–91.

[96] Precisely what Calvin also believed: Robert Letham, *Systematic Theology* (Wheaton, IL.: Crossway, 2019), 787.

[97] From Book 2 of his *Answer* to Gardiner, in Cox, *Works 1*, 183. Cranmer was introduced to Chrysostom by Bucer (Chapman, *Anglican Theology*, 36).

And in another place he saith: 'Why dost thou prepare thy belly and thy teeth? Believe, and thou hast eaten.'[98]

Cranmer, then, would not have us attach some mystical or magical property to the Supper itself. It is not a work that saves us, but a sign and a nourishment of the union believers have already with Christ by the Spirit:

> But we say, that the presence of Christ in his holy supper is a spiritual presence: and as he is spiritually present, so is he spiritually eaten of all faithful christian men, not only when they receive the sacrament, but continually so long as they be members spiritual of Christ's mystical body. And... doth Christ feed us so long as we dwell in him and he in us, and not only when we receive the sacrament.[99]

The Lord's Supper, then, is 'a present moment in which the Spirit of God acts on the hearts of believers by faith ("and feed on him in your heart by faith with thanksgiving"). That's why Cranmer called the sacrament "Holy Communion."'[100]

As ever, Cranmer would not have claimed that his theology of the Supper was anything novel. Quite the opposite: one is struck by the sheer proliferation of references to and quotations of the Church Fathers in his *Answer* to Gardiner, and recent research has showed Cranmer's indebtedness to Cyril of Alexandria as regards the work of the Spirit at the Supper.[101] Cranmer also collaborated closely with Bucer and Vermigli – themselves formidable patristic scholars – on his

---

[98] From Book 4 of his *Answer* to Gardiner, in Cox, *Works 1*, 208. Note the similarity of language to Article XXIX of the Thirty-Nine Articles – not written by Cranmer but clearly articulating his theology (see, for example, Bray, *The Faith We Confess*, 167–69).

[99] From the *Answer* to Gardiner, Book 2, in Cox, *Works 1*, 71. In Book 3, Cranmer wrote: 'Cyril and Hilary entreat both of one matter, that we be united together and with Christ, not only in will, but also in nature, and be made one, not only in consent of godly religion, but also that Christ, taking our corporal nature upon him, hath made us partakers of his godly nature, knitting us together with him unto his Father and to his Holy Spirit', 169.

[100] Michael Jensen, 'Sola Fide,' in Null and Yates, *Reformation Anglicanism*, 140.

[101] Jensen, *Reformation Anglican Worship*, 115.

theology of the Supper, and on the Communion liturgy.[102] The three men were united in rejecting Luther's idea of consubstantiation and Zwinglian memorialist theology: they were much closer to Calvin's teaching.[103] Some of Vermigli's comments in particular show his close affinity with Cranmer:

> As believers both eat and drink the bread and wine with bodily mouth, so their souls are stirred up by the favour of the Holy Spirit, the words of God and the outward symbols, and are carried to heaven, reaching all the way to Christ with the mouth of faith.[104]

Martyr also taught that the 'symbols are not only signs of the body and blood of Christ, but also instruments which the Holy Spirit uses to feed us spiritually with the body and blood of the Lord.'[105]

Thus, we may be confident that Cranmer's view on the sacrament was a thoroughly Reformed, and a thoroughly Trinitarian one. Perhaps it is best summarised in his own words: 'we receive spiritual feeding and supernatural nourishment from heaven, of the very true body and blood of our Saviour Christ, through the omnipotent power of God, and the wonderful working of the Holy Ghost.'[106] Once again, however, Cranmer's particular achievement was to articulate this Reformed theology in his liturgy, so that all members of the Church might understand and rejoice.[107]

---

[102] Nick Needham comments: 'none of the first or second generation Reformers was so intellectually and spiritually drenched in the fathers as Martyr, except perhaps Bucer, Calvin and Cranmer.' Nick Needham, 'Peter Martyr and the Eucharistic Controversy,' *SBET* 17 (1999): 11.

[103] For a more thorough exploration, see Basil Hall, 'Cranmer, the Eucharist and the Foreign Divines in the Reign of Edward VI,' in Ayris and Selwyn, *Thomas Cranmer: Churchman and Scholar,* 217–58; also Chapman, *Anglican Theology,* 31–38.

[104] The quotation is from Vermigli's 'Letters on the Eucharist,' cited by Sung Ho Lee, 'Peter Martyr Vermigli's View of Faith and the Holy Spirit in the Eucharist,' *Reform & Revival* 23 (2019): 82–83.

[105] Needham, 'Eucharistic Controversy,' 12.

[106] From Book 2 of the *Answer* to Gardiner, in Cox, *Works 1,* 71. Somewhat convolutedly, Cranmer is refuting a misreading of a book that his opponents wrongly (in his opinion) attributed to St Ambrose.

[107] We do not have space to explore Cranmer's theology of baptism here, but a thoughtful reading of the 1552 baptism services will reveal the same Trinitarian patterns (as seen in the quotation above, on p. 24). Cranmer tightly linked

The Importance of the Trinity to Cranmer

To summarise, how important did Cranmer consider the doctrine of the Trinity to be? It should be clear that for Cranmer, Christian worship is Trinitarian worship – explicitly and consciously so. Anything else is quite simply not in agreement with the historic Christian faith. Before moving on to consider Cranmer's Trinitarian legacy, I will briefly add two further pieces of evidence. First, Canon 5 of the *Reformatio Legum Ecclesiasticarum*, states that 'virtually all things which pertain to the catholic faith (both as regards the most blessed Trinity and as regards the mysteries of our redemption) are briefly contained in the three creeds'.[108] For Cranmer, the true catholic faith comprises both the Trinity and our redemption. We cannot have a Christian faith without the Trinity, any more than we can have a Christian faith without redemption.

Secondly, and most movingly, are the words of Cranmer's final prayer:

> And here, kneeling down, he said: 'O Father of heaven, O Son of God, Redeemer of the world, O Holy Ghost, proceeding from them both, three Persons and one God, have mercy upon me... Thou didst not give thy Son unto death for small sins only, but for all and the greatest sins of the world... I crave nothing, O Lord, for mine own merits, but for thy name's sake, that it may be hallowed thereby, and for thy dear Son, Jesus Christ's sake'.[109]

---

baptism to the Supper: 'For Christ teacheth that we receive very bread and wine in the most blessed supper of the Lord, as sacraments to admonish us, that as we be fed with bread and wine bodily, so we be fed with the body and blood of our Saviour Christ spiritually: as in our baptism we receive very water, to signify unto us, that as water is an element to wash the body outwardly, so be our souls washed by the Holy Ghost inwardly.' Book 1 of his *Answer* to Gardiner, in Cox, *Works 1*, 46. See Null, *Repentance*, 227–31, for Cranmer's views on baptism and his theological agreement with Vermigli.

[108] In Bray, *Tudor Church Reform*, 173–75. The title is *Of the Three Creeds*. Again, this corresponds very closely to Article XII of the Forty-Two (XIII of the Thirty-Nine), but the Article does not contain the reference to the Trinity.

[109] In Cox, *Works 1*, xxvi. Cox is quoting from Foxe's *Book of Martyrs*. There are a few slightly differing versions of Cranmer's final speech (see MacCulloch, *Cranmer*, 601, fn 116), but his prayer at the beginning of it is very much the same across them all.

Here, Cranmer is about to refute his recantation of the Reformed faith: these words come shortly before his famous comments about holding his offending hand first to the flames. He confesses that this 'one thing grieveth my conscience more than all the rest' – and so he casts himself on the mercy of Father, Son and Spirit. The Archbishop did exactly what he taught (and continues to teach) countless multitudes to do: at the hour of his death, Cranmer worshipped, loved and trusted in the Triune God.

This is an appropriate place to conclude with some reflections on the Trinitarian legacy which Cranmer has left us.

4. Cranmer's Trinitarian Legacy

'Glory be to the Father, and to the Son, and to the Holy Ghost. As it was in the beginning, is now, and ever shall be: world without end. Amen.' Surely no doxology is more familiar to the English-speaking world. Cranmer did not write it, he was not the first to include it in a liturgical prayer book, nor was he the first to translate medieval liturgy into English.[1] But there is no doubt that Cranmer was the architect of and mastermind behind the *BCP* as we have it. Its shape and style are irrefutably his: 'Whatever help... Cranmer received, he should take credit for the overall job of editorship and the overarching structure of the book.'[2] It is Cranmer, as Archbishop, who ensured that this doxology was included in the *BCP* – along with the Creeds and countless other Trinitarian prayers – for all English-speaking believers to pray in their own language. The effect (both conscious and unconscious) of Cranmer's liturgy on English language, literature and theology is difficult to overstate:

> Cranmer could not know in 1552 that he was providing a vehicle for English worship which would remain unchanged for four hundred years; with his natural modesty and restraint, he might have been appalled... Cranmer's prose has done much to guide the direction of the English language... Cranmer deserves the gratitude not merely of the Church of England, but of all English speakers throughout the world.[3]

This is as true of his articulation of the Trinity as of anything else. MacCulloch observes that 'it remains open to question as to whether Cranmer regarded the 1552 rite as his final word.'[4] It is possible that Cranmer would have revised some of the phrasing around the Communion service. However, we can be confident that his doctrine of the Trinity would not have changed; it did not do so between 1549

---

[1] MacCulloch, *Cranmer*, 418, notes that Robert Redman did so in 1535. MacCulloch observes that 'If [Cranmer] were writing liturgy today, he would face crippling lawsuits for breach of copyright', 631.
[2] MacCulloch, *Cranmer*, 417. MacCulloch makes this remark about the 1549 *BCP*, but it applies equally well to the 1552.
[3] MacCulloch, *Cranmer*, 630–31. See 606–32 for MacCulloch's reflections on Cranmer.
[4] MacCulloch, *Cranmer*, 511.

and 1552, nor had it in the preceding years. Neither the Elizabethan 1559 nor the Restoration 1662 *BCPs* altered the Trinitarian aspects in any notable way. Ever since, the Trinitarian nature of the *BCP* has been recognised and (by many) treasured. In this final section, I will briefly consider some historical aspects of Cranmer's Trinitarian legacy and conclude with some final lessons for our own day.

Historical Influence

We may trace Cranmer's influence across Anglican (and wider) history. The *Second Book of Homilies,* most likely written by Bishop John Jewel, is clearly indebted to Cranmer's Trinitarian theology in many places: for instance, on prayer and on the Holy Spirit. The same is true of the writings of other early Anglican theologians, like Hooker.[5] Almost a century after Cranmer, the Laudians of the 1640s were concerned that the loss of the *BCP* would mean the loss of the doctrine of the Trinity. One of them, Edmund Porter:

> ... offered a blistering rebuke of the Presbyterians, Independents, and other groups who sought to eliminate the Book of Common Prayer from parish worship. Porter's point was as simple as stinging: do away with the Church of England, do away with the Prayer Book, and then the entire edifice of trinitarian faith falls apart, notwithstanding the most laudable and indefatigable trinitarian efforts of the Puritans.[6]

We should note that on one level, Cranmer would disagree thoroughly with Porter: the Trinitarian faith does not stand or fall by his liturgy, but rests on the Scriptures. So long as they are faithfully preached, the Trinity will be known. As we have seen, Scripture, not the *BCP*, is the instrument through which the triune God dwells with his church, and the church with him. But the Laudians correctly recognised how the *BCP* could play a crucial role in ensuring that the doctrine of the Trinity was widely proclaimed and upheld among the people: this of course was precisely Cranmer's aim. The Laudians were right to be concerned that the *BCP* might be lost. At the same time, at the other end of the theological spectrum, the Westminster Assembly rejected much of

---

[5] See, for example, Jensen, *Reformation Anglican Worship*, 140–48.
[6] Paul C. H. Lim, *Mystery Unveiled: The Crisis of the Trinity in Early Modern England* (Oxford: Oxford University Press, 2012), 137.

Cranmer's *BCP* structure. However, chapter II of the Westminster Confession, *Of God, and of the Holy Trinity*, declares:

> There is but one only, living, and true God: ...without body, parts, or passions ... In the unity of the Godhead there be three persons, of one substance, power, and eternity; God the Father, God the Son, and God the Holy Ghost. The Father is of none, neither begotten, nor proceeding: the Son is eternally begotten of the Father: the Holy Ghost eternally proceeding from the Father and the Son.[7]

The phrase 'but one... living and true God... without body, parts, or passions' is verbatim from Cranmer's Article I.[8]

Meanwhile, John Bunyan added his own rather uncomplimentary voice to the discussion. Bunyan would not have disagreed with Cranmer on the essential doctrine of the Trinity, but he was a passionate anti-liturgist: 'Those prayers in the Common Prayer-book, was such as made by other men, and not by the motions of the Holy Ghost... The Scripture... doth not say the *Common Prayer-book* teacheth us how to pray, but the Spirit.'[9]

Thankfully, however, Bunyan's views on the *BCP* did not prevail. Its influence did not abate – rather, it continued and increased, shaping the thought of Christian leaders in the following centuries. Seng-Kong Tan notes that '[John] Wesley's profound yet practical, metrical theology of the Trinity is deeply anchored in the Anglican Prayer Book tradition, with particular indebtedness to the ecumenical creeds of Nicaea and Athanasius.'[10] Wesley's near contemporary John Newton was clearly

---

[7] The Westminster Confession of Faith may be viewed online at: https://www.ligonier.org/learn/articles/the-westminster-confession-of-faith-1647. Notice the presence of *Filioque* here. Westminster, in common with several other Reformed explanations of the faith, but in contrast to Cranmer, began with the Scriptures rather than with the Trinity.

[8] As we have seen, this phraseology was not entirely original to Cranmer – although the arrangement and translation to English was (Bray, *The Faith We Confess*, 9, 19).

[9] Quoted in Michael A. G. Haykin, 'The Holy Spirit and Prayer in John Bunyan,' *Reformation and Revival* 3, no. 2 (Spring 1994): 86. John Owen held similar views.

[10] Seng-Kong Tan, 'The Doctrine of the Trinity in John Wesley's Prose and Poetic Works,' *Journal for Christian Theological Research* 7 (2002): 4. Wesley, a

unimpressed with many of the attempted explanations of the Trinity in his day, commenting in a letter to a fellow clergyman: 'I have seen laboured defences of the Trinity, which have given me not much more satisfaction than I should probably receive from a dissertation upon the rainbow, composed by a man blind from his birth.'[11] However, as a good Anglican, Newton knew where to turn for doctrinally and devotionally satisfying 'defences of the Trinity'! In the following century, Charles Simeon declared of the *BCP*: 'The repeated cries to each Person of the ever-adorable Trinity for mercy, are not at all too frequent or too fervent for me...'[12] It is not hard to detect Cranmer's influence in John Stott's 'daily Trinity prayer:

> Good morning heavenly Father, good morning Lord Jesus, good morning Holy Spirit. Heavenly Father, I worship you as the creator and sustainer of the universe. Lord Jesus, I worship you, Savior and Lord of the world. Holy Spirit, I worship you, sanctifier of the people of God. Glory to the Father, and to the Son and to the Holy Spirit. Heavenly Father, I pray that I may live this day in your presence and please you more and more. Lord Jesus, I pray that this day I may take up my cross and follow you. Holy Spirit, I pray that this day you will fill me with yourself and cause your fruit to ripen in my life: love, joy, peace, patience, kindness, goodness, faithfulness, gentleness and self-control. Holy, blessed and glorious Trinity, three persons in one God, have mercy upon me. Amen.[13]

---

prominent preacher and revivalist in the eighteenth century, was the son of an Anglican clergyman.

[11] *The Works of John Newton vol. 1* (Edinburgh: Banner of Truth, 2015; repr. 2018), 416. Evidently, questionable illustrations for the Trinity are not a modern phenomenon.

[12] Handley Moule, *Charles Simeon* (London: Methuen, 1892), 214, quoted in Packer, *Gospel in the Prayer Book*, 3. Simeon, the 'preacher of a famous set of University sermons on The Excellency of the Liturgy, never lost an opportunity of praising the Prayer Book and criticizing its critics.' Packer, *Gospel in the Prayer Book*, 1.

[13] Quoted in Trevin Wax, 'John Stott's Morning Trinitarian Prayer': https://www.thegospelcoalition.org/blogs/trevin-wax/john-stotts-morning-trinitarian-prayer/.

We could find many more such examples of Cranmer's influence on notable ministers, leaders and theologians. This is not to mention the multitudes of churchgoers since the Reformation who have had their theology in this area shaped by Cranmer, nor indeed the impact of the *BCP* on wider English, later British, culture as a whole.[14] (Indeed, it was not until 1813 that the legal penalties for those who denied the doctrine of the Trinity were removed from British law.)[15] Since 1662, the *BCP* has been through numerous subsequent English editions and revisions. Many of these have continued to (more or less) articulate Cranmer's doctrine of the Trinity. Even the much-debated *Alternative Service Book* of 1980 retained a basic Trinitarian structure, as does *Common Worship*.[16] Assent to the historic Trinitarian faith is still officially required for positions of leadership within the Church of England.

The impact of the *BCP* was of course not limited to the British Isles. As the global reach of Britain increased, it was Cranmer's articulation of the Trinity that spread across much of the world. Men like Captain Cook sailed with the *BCP* on board, and as British territories became established, it was the Reformed, Anglican expression of Christianity that became embedded in the minds of huge numbers of people. We may debate the merits or otherwise of the British Empire, and we should also note that those who carried the *BCP* across the Empire were not necessarily Reformed in their own theology (some were Anglo-Catholic, others, like Cook, were at very best nominal in their Christian faith). Britain's global influence was, however, undoubtedly the channel through which countless people came under the sound of the Trinitarian gospel. Cummings captures some of the tension of this global expansion: '*The Book of Common Prayer* spread with the reach of colonial ambition, so that just as the sun never set, so Evensong

---

[14] For some reflections, especially in the area of language, see MacCulloch, *Cranmer*, 630–32.

[15] The House of Commons notes for 5 May 1813, on the 'Bill for the Relief of Persons Denying the Doctrine of the Trinity': https://babel.hathitrust.org/cgi/pt?id=uc1.$b333360&view=1up&seq=586&skin=2021.

[16] However, 'The biggest change in *Common Worship* lay not in replacing the *Book of Common Prayer* outright, as its many defenders feared, but in abolishing its uniformity... Congregations are encouraged to experiment and improvise in ways which would have shocked Cranmer, and horrified Laud.' Brian Cummings, *The Book of Common Prayer: A Very Short Introduction* (Oxford: Oxford University Press, 2018), 102. The dangers (from a Trinitarian perspective) of allowing a free liturgical hand will become clear below.

never ended in the British Empire.'[17] This included the translation of the *BCP* into other languages: Urdu in 1814, Maori in 1830 and Swahili in 1876, for example.[18] Chloë Starr has written a fascinating analysis of the nineteenth-century efforts to translate the *BCP* into Chinese. Robert Morrison, a Presbyterian, recognised the importance of the Creeds, along with Morning and Evening Prayer, and laboured to translate their statements concerning the triune God into consistent, clear Chinese (although in his early efforts, he did not attempt to translate the Athanasian Creed – perhaps understandably).[19] His efforts bore fruit as the *BCP* took hold: a Chinese preface to the later *Prayer Book for All*, 'presents basic theology, such as a précis of the Trinity... Psalms and collects, explain the editors, laud the Trinity and express God's unfathomable *dao de*.'[20] Translations into other languages could not exactly reduplicate Cranmer's poetic style, but they could (and did) communicate his theology. Today, across the English-speaking world, millions still articulate Cranmer's teaching on the Trinity week by week; it is still imprinted on countless minds and hearts. His Trinitarian legacy is truly vast.

Contemporary Concerns

'Contemporary Anglicans,' observes D. A. Carson, are 'often awash in doctrinal and moral confusion.'[21] This is certainly true in the area of Trinitarian theology (as is shown by a current Archbishop's curious reference to 'a United Kingdom, four countries in one nation, a fascinating Trinitarian model of nationhood itself').[22] Here I shall reflect on some areas of ongoing confusion in Trinitarian doctrine.

---

[17] Cummings, *Book of Common Prayer*, 99.

[18] Cummings, *Book of Common Prayer*, 98–99. The American colonies saw Mohawk *BCPs* in the eighteenth century, and, after Independence, a 1789 *BCP* (90–97). Sadly, the American *BCPs* of 1789 and, later, 1928 and 1979, did not include the Athanasian Creed for use in public worship. The *BCP* was also translated into Welsh in the 1560s (88).

[19] Chloë Starr, 'The Prayer Book in Nineteenth-Century China,' *Monumenta Serica* 56 (2008): 395–426. See especially 407–8, 416–19, on the challenges of divine names.

[20] Starr, *Prayer Book in Nineteenth-Century China*, 421.

[21] This quotation is taken from D. A. Carson's endorsement of Null and Yates, *Reformation Anglicanism*, 1.

[22] Stephen Cottrell, *Dear England* (London: Hodder & Stoughton, 2022), 148. At the time of writing, Cottrell is the Archbishop of York. In fairness, we should note that Cottrell is on much firmer ground earlier in the book: 'When Christians speak about God their most profoundly important...language

First, there has been pressure in recent decades from the Eastern Church for the *filioque* clause to be removed from Anglican liturgy. Some have responded to this by doing so: the Anglican Church of Canada (ACC) have removed the clause from their version of the Nicene Creed, while the Synod declared: 'This action implies no change in the doctrine expressed in Article V of the Thirty-Nine Articles contained in the Book of Common Prayer'.[23] It is very unlikely that Cranmer would have agreed with this sentiment.[24] As we have seen, Canon 2 of the *Reformatio Legum Ecclesiasticarum* is most insistent on the *filioque*, and Cranmer inserted it into the Litany, along with several other references to it in the *BCP*. The Western Church, Cranmer included, held that there are good Scriptural grounds for the *filioque*. Centuries of Western reflection on the procession of persons, and on the connection of this to God's self-revelation, should not be too quickly dismissed. The removal of the *filioque* undoubtedly implies shift in perspective and understanding, if not core doctrine.[25] It is right that in one sense we regard this as a 'non-primary' concern. The *filioque* is not a theological hill for Anglicans to die on and Christians may disagree in unity here. But Anglican leaders and teachers should be confident that the *filioque* is theologically defensible and be prepared to teach others so. At the very least, Anglicans need to know our own historic theology, lest we become deeply confused. Gerald Bray is right:

> ...the message for Anglicans is clear: there is an urgent need for them to rediscover their own theology, and to examine its true relationship, not only to the Greek Fathers (as seen through western eyes) but to the reality of modern Orthodoxy. Only when this has

---

concerns a description of God as community: the one who is known to us as Father, Son and Holy Spirit... [w]ithin God, therefore, there is a giving and receiving of love within a community of persons. It is from this giving and receiving of love that creation flows...' Cottrell, *Dear England*, 46.

[23] Quoted in Craig, '*Filioque* Clause,' 421. The ACC version of the Nicene Creed may be viewed online: https://www.anglican.ca/about/beliefs/nicene-creed/.

[24] Granting, of course, that Cranmer did not write Article V. But he most certainly was in accord with its theology.

[25] Letham remarks on 'recent attempts to paper over the cracks by claiming that there has been no real divergence between the East and West on the Trinity. A millennium or more of church history cannot be ignored or swept under the carpet.' Robert Letham, *Through Western Eyes: Eastern Orthodoxy: A Western Perspective* (Fearn, Ross-shire: Christian Focus, 2007), 224. See 224–42 for discussion, in addition to the section in *The Holy Trinity* mentioned above.

been adequately done will Anglican theologians be in a position to conduct serious and realistic discussions of the *filioque* (and of other matters which divide us) on a level of theological analysis appropriate both to the gravity of the issues involved and to the significance which the Orthodox have consistently attached to them.[26]

Much more serious has been the blurring and obscuring of Trinitarian theology in recent liturgical revisions. As an example, consider a publication named *Enriching our Worship 1: Morning and Evening Prayer, The Great Litany, and The Holy Eucharist (EOW1)*.[27] This is intended as a supplement to the existing (US) Episcopal Church *BCP*. The Preface declares: 'At all points along the way in the process of selection and development of texts the question has been asked: Is this text consistent with the Trinitarian and Christological formulations which we, as Anglicans, regard as normative and the ground of our common prayer?'[28] This is an excellent foundation from which to start. Sadly, though, our answer to the question must be negative. The *filioque* clause is removed, for the rather concerning reason that 'Whether or not to restore the original wording of the Nicene Creed is not primarily a theological issue. The relation of the Holy Spirit to

---

[26] Gerald Bray, 'Filioque and Anglican-Orthodox Dialogue,' *Churchman* 93 (1979): 134. Bray is also helpful in a recent comment: 'The issues at stake are hard for many people to grasp, but that does not mean that they are unimportant. The Western churches cannot simply drop the *Filioque* clause, because to do so would have unintended consequences for their theology, but neither do they wish to use it as a weapon against the Eastern churches. On the whole, it seems that most Anglicans, like other Westerners, are prepared to agree that there are different ways of looking at the Trinity, and that the Eastern formula has a validity within its own frame of reference.' Gerald Bray, *Anglicanism: A Reformed Catholic Tradition* (Bellingham, WA: Lexham, 2021), 69. By contrast, while Craig's discussion has much that is helpful, we cannot agree with his conclusion: 'Simply put, if it would give the West less pain to remove the clause than it gives the East to have it remain, it were better removed...It is clear that, even if the *Filioque* is removed from the text of the Creed, there is no danger that any part of our heritage will be lost.' (Craig, '*Filioque* Clause,' 438–39).
[27] The Church Pension Fund. *Enriching our Worship 1: Morning and Evening Prayer, The Great Litany, and The Holy Eucharist* (New York, NY: Church Publishing, 1998). Further editions of this series have covered other parts of liturgy.
[28] *EOW1*, 5–6.

the first and second persons of the Holy Trinity remains a matter of theological discussion and is ultimately unknowable.'[29] It will not do to simply throw our hands up and say, 'We do not and cannot know.' Further, while the liturgy regularly refers to 'The holy and undivided Trinity, one God,' all references to 'three persons' have been expunged. This is problematic: God cannot be Trinity if he is not three persons, and if the Trinity is generically referred to as 'God,' modalism is rearing its head. While some Trinitarian elements are maintained in *EOW1* (for example, the creeds), it is distinctly ambiguous on the full deity of the Son and Spirit. In a thorough study, Matthew Olver writes, 'there is also nothing in *EOW1* – especially the eucharistic prayers – that precludes a subordinationist trinitarian theology.'[30] While occasional petition is offered to Christ, he could be some form of demigod, or a highly exalted saint. Far from enriching our worship, a liturgy that is sub-Trinitarian is not Christian worship at all.

EOW1 also displays another trend in recent decades towards addressing God as 'Creator, Redeemer, Sanctifier' (or something similar), rather than as Father, Son and Holy Spirit.[31] The Litany in *EOW1* begins: 'Holy God, Creator of heaven and earth, Have mercy on us. Holy and Mighty, Redeemer of the world, Have mercy on us. Holy Immortal One, Sanctifier of the faithful, Have mercy on us. Holy, blessed and glorious Trinity, One God, Have mercy on us.'[32] This is theologically adequate as far as it goes, but the problem is what is absent: the names of the persons have been removed. The contrast with Cranmer's opening sentences (quoted earlier) is startling. Cranmer certainly approves of ascribing particular works to the particular persons of Trinity; but he most definitely will not allow us to *substitute* the works for the persons. This constitutes a grievous theological misstep, as David Sellery helpfully summarises:

> This way of describing God is as inadequate and misleading... because it replaces the persons of the Trinity by their functions. This heresy is also known as Economic Trinitarianism because it implies that there are merely three operations within the economy of salvation rather than three eternal persons within the

---

[29] *EOW1*, 76.
[30] Matthew S. C. Olver, 'The Eucharistic Materials in *Enriching Our Worship 1: A Consideration of its Trinitarian Theology,' *ATR* 98 (2016): 668.
[31] See Letham, *Systematic Theology*, 162–63 for an overview.
[32] *EOW1*, 46.

Godhead. This is not the Christian faith we confess in the Nicene Creed.[33]

This blurring of persons and functions has sadly led to confusion in some Anglican circles as to who God actually is. A recent Church of England video asked various members of the Church the question: 'how would you describe who God is?'[34] Though a couple of interviewees responded with Trinitarian replies, many of the answers were given (more or less confidently) in terms of *what God does* in relation to his creation (his love, presence, friendship and so forth) – not *who God is*. Of course, God's work of creation and redemption is glorious, as is the way he relates to his people. All of this flows out from who he is as a Trinity of persons, and it is rightly celebrated – Cranmer both knew and taught so. However, Cranmer would not have us confuse persons and works. Believing that God *is* the way he relates to us, apart from being theologically muddled, opens us to the danger of believing that God somehow revolves around (or is even dependent upon) his creatures.[35] Anyone who has fed richly on a diet of Cranmer's liturgy will recoil from such a notion: the *BCP* teaches us that God *is* Father, Son and Holy Spirit, the eternal, uncreated Trinity, who does not need us but has freely come to us in his gracious love. Such a God, far from being dependent upon us, is instead worthy of all our worship, as we have seen. Cranmer will not allow us to think otherwise for a moment.

Once we have taken the step away from allowing God himself to tell us who he is, we are on a theological slippery slope. This is demonstrated by a recent and concerning movement in some Anglican circles to refer to God as 'she' or 'Mother.'[36] Maternal liturgy features in *EOW1*, but has become even more pronounced in subsequent years. Indeed, as I write this (Spring 2023), the Church of England is considering 'a

---

[33] David Sellery, 'We Believe in One God: Father, Son, and Holy Spirit,' *Churchman* 106 (1992): 161. Sellery has a number of useful reflections in this article.

[34] Available online: https://www.churchofengland.org/our-faith/what-we-believe. Strikingly, the text on this webpage explains the Christian faith in solidly Trinitarian (and Anglican) terms. Perhaps this serves as a reminder that we need our Trinitarian faith not merely written on webpages, but boldly preached, prayed, spoken and sung in our churches – see below.

[35] Precisely the problem which Islam faces – Reeves, *The Good God*, 22.

[36] See, for example, Nadia Khomami, 'Let God be a "she", says Church of England women's group': https://www.theguardian.com/world/2015/jun/01/church-of-england-womens-group-bishops.

new joint project on gendered language.'[37] Given the direction that other liberalising denominations have gone in recently, it would not be surprising to see the Church of England adopt maternal or generic language (for example, 'God our Parent') into its liturgy. Recent suggestions for alternative Holy Week liturgy include phrases such as 'the example of our mother, Jesus' and the responsive prayer 'Mother, have mercy.'[38] This would be a tragedy, and a disaster: it is very far removed from Cranmer's language – which, of course, is not simply Cranmer's language at all, but that of God himself, speaking in the Scriptures. Olver notes that Aquinas can help us here: he distinguished carefully between metaphor and proper names. The Scriptures sometimes speak of God as being *like* a mother – for example, 'As a mother comforts her child, so will I comfort you; and you will be comforted over Jerusalem' (Isa 66:13 NIVUK). Olver continues: 'In God, however, "paternity" speaks of who the First Person *is:* the eternal begetter of the Son and the spirator of the Spirit.'[39] 'Father' is not a metaphor: it is who the Father *is*. Cranmer knew so. If we wish to be faithful to the way in which God has revealed himself to us – and so avoid idolatry – we must follow Cranmer's example . As Jensen says:

> In the twentieth century, prayer book revisions have frequently altered the terms of address for God, seeking, on the one hand, to minimize the emphasis on the divine power and, on the other, to gender-neutralize the language of 'Father.' Both of these tendencies are sadly misguided and potentially very dangerous for Christian faith, since prayer to a powerless God is of no comfort at all, and prayer to a God who is not the Father of Jesus Christ is not Christian prayer... He is Father because he is the Father of Jesus, the brother of Christians. He is Father because he is the Father of many prodigal children, whom he welcomes with tender and loving arms back into the fold.[40]

[37] PA Media, 'Church of England to consider use of gender-neutral terms for God': https://www.theguardian.com/world/2023/feb/07/church-of-england-to-consider-use-of-gender-neutral-terms-for-god.

[38] These examples are provided by Women and the Church, and can be found at: https://womenandthechurch.org/resources/liturgical-writings-2020/.

[39] Olver, 'Trinitarian Theology,' 671, and see the discussion, 670–72. Spiration is 'The defining characteristic of the Holy Spirit, who proceeds from (or is breathed out by) the Father.' Letham, *Holy Spirit*, 306.

[40] Jensen, *Reformation Anglican Worship*, 147–48.

It is also worth noting Scott Swain's comments with reference to Vermigli, Cranmer's friend and colleague:

> Early Protestant catechetical texts also regularly distinguish the Trinitarian persons *ad intra* from their works *ad extra*: 'We should… distinguish between the Spirit and the works he does or the gifts he gives', Vermigli insists in his 1544 commentary on the Apostles' Creed… Yet it is not only the distinction but also the relationship between the persons and their works that reveals the rich Trinitarian piety of Reformation era catechesis. In response to the question concerning why we call God 'Father', Vermigli provides two reasons: 'first, because he is the Father of Jesus Christ our Lord, the second person of the Godhead; the other reason is that it has pleased him to be called our Father, since he shares with us both likeness and inheritance.'[41]

Cranmer would have us be clear; we must worship God as he has revealed himself to be: Father, Son and Holy Spirit.

Moving somewhat closer to home (from my perspective), evangelicals too are guilty of Trinitarian confusion, particularly in the areas of prayer and the Lord's Supper. I will reflect briefly on these in turn.

It is worth noting that Cranmer has left us a book of *common prayer*. Historically speaking, most Christians have either not been able to afford their own Bible or have not been able to read (or both). This was true in Cranmer's sixteenth-century England.[42] It is easy for us to forget how dramatic a change near-universal literacy has brought. For example, the 'quiet time' of private Bible reading has been something of a pillar of recent Western evangelicalism. This has undoubtedly been a great blessing to many (myself included), but we should remember

---

[41] Scott R. Swain, 'The Trinity in the Reformers,' in *The Oxford Handbook of the Trinity*, ed. Gilles Emery O.P. and Matthew Levering (Oxford: Oxford University Press, 2011), 236.

[42] It is difficult to be precise about literacy rates in Tudor England, and of course they varied greatly across regions and social classes, but most estimate that the average literacy rate was somewhere around 20% for men, and 10% for women. (See, for example, the comments of one recent historian: https://www.bookbrunch.co.uk/page/free-article/the-british-and-reading-a-short-history/;.

that in terms of church history it is a rather modern anomaly.[43] In Cranmer's thinking, while a priest is charged to read the Scriptures diligently at his ordination ('Will you be diligent in prayers, and in reading of the holy scriptures...?' the Bishop asks), the *BCP* does not command all believers to be individually reading the Scriptures. Of course, Cranmer wanted all believers to *know* the Scriptures: that is why his liturgy is so full of them, and why ministers are so strictly charged to know and teach them clearly. But to expect many to read the Bible by themselves was unrealistic. Prayer, however, is something common to all Christians. It was Trinitarian prayer which Cranmer considered to be the supreme expression of Christian faith.

It is a real shame then, that evangelical and/or Reformed Anglican churches have become so muddled in this area. Perhaps we have done the opposite to Cranmer: we have been good at exhorting people to personal Bible reading, and in training church members how to read the Bible, but I do not think we have done so well at helping people to pray in a Trinitarian way. For example, too often, one will hear a prayer expressing thanks to the Father for dying on the cross for us, or a reference to the Holy Spirit as 'it.' This is deeply inaccurate – not to say heretical – and most certainly falls foul of the 'neither confounding the persons nor dividing the substance' against which the Athanasian Creed warns us. It would not be unfair to say that modalism is widespread in some Anglican evangelical circles: many think of God – and so pray to him – as a rather nebulous 'Lord,' rather than addressing him as the almighty and merciful Father (in the name of his precious Son, by his powerful Holy Spirit), as the *BCP* instructs us to do. All of this is of course largely subconscious and unintentional, but that is rather the point: one of the reasons for it is that we use so little of our historic liturgy. Anglicans have never been against extempore prayer, but this is now vastly more common than liturgical prayer in many evangelical Anglican circles (at least, in England; it must be admitted that Reformed Anglicans in other provinces do rather better). In some cases, this has led – contrary to Bunyan's fears – to prayer that is further removed from the Bible's teaching rather than closer to it. If Anglicans wish to think of and speak to our triune God in a way that honours how he has revealed himself to us, and that indeed brings joy to us, then

---

[43] I suspect that in many British conservative evangelical churches, one of the first answers to a question such as 'how do you grow as a Christian?' will be a (perhaps rather guilty) 'I need to read my Bible more!'

Cranmer's precisely constructed, beautifully expressed liturgy would be of immeasurable help. As Letham comments:

> Many of the great prayers of the Christian church are steeped in trinitarian teaching. Foremost among these is the great *Te Deum*. The Collects in *The Book of Common Prayer* express the church's relationship to the triune God; these prayers impress themselves on the memories of congregants. Not only do they provide a springboard for refreshing the prayers of individuals when they find it difficult to pray, but they also contain a nucleus of trinitarian expressions that can be internalized in the minds of the faithful.[44]

Cranmer's prayers teach us who God is and what God is like: surely no need is greater than for Anglicans to remember and rejoice in these things. Greater use of the Collects or other set prayers during services, prayer meetings, Bible studies, committees and conferences would not go amiss. We could do little better than to once again allow the great Archbishop to teach us how to pray.

In addition to prayer, Anglicans could work to apply the *BCP*'s Trinitarian principles to corporate church life, in areas such as singing and preaching.[45] The Trinitarian patterns in the ordering services, and their connection to the preaching of the word, are unmissable. For example, at the end of *The Form of Consecrating of an Archbishop or Bishop*, the presiding minister prays:

> Most merciful Father, we beseech thee to send down upon this thy servant, thy heavenly blessing, and so endue him with thy Holy Spirit, that he preaching thy word... at the latter day he may receive the crown of righteousness, laid up by the Lord... who liveth and reigneth, one God, with the Father and Holy Ghost, world without end. Amen.

There is also a very pertinent application here to the celebration of the Lord's Supper. In general, the West has become a very audio-visual culture: people prefer to listen or watch rather than to read. We may

---

[44] Robert Letham, 'The Trinity and worship,' in *The Essential Trinity: New Testament Foundations and Practices*, eds. Brandon D. Crowe and Carl R. Trueman (London: Apollos, 2016), 254.
[45] Note the comments in Letham, *Trinity*, 496.

debate the merits or defects of this, but it remains a fact, and in some ways it actually brings us closer to Cranmer's England. I believe that this makes a revived appreciation and use of the Supper even more critical.

Anglican evangelicals can often have a distressingly low view of Holy Communion, a far cry from Cranmer's 'ultimate expression of... God's gracious love inspiring human love... which he intended to be the central act of English worship.'[46] We may not quite agree that the Supper is the 'ultimate expression' or the 'central act' of corporate worship.[47] But in our (very right) efforts to place a high value on the preaching of the word and perhaps to avoid unhealthy ritualism, I believe we have swung too far and have devalued a precious gift from the Lord. Indeed, in some evangelical Anglican churches, unfortunately the Supper can feel rather like a monthly 'add-on' to the Sunday service, one that lengthens proceedings, delaying coffee by ten (or more) somewhat mysterious minutes. Certainly in my experience, it is not common for the Lord's Supper to be included in essential or basic doctrinal instruction courses, nor to feature to any great extent in congregational preaching and teaching.[48]

Were it to be explained and understood that at the Supper, communicants are being raised by the Spirit to the heavens to feed on Christ in the love of the Father, and that we may indeed 'lift up our hearts' to the Lord by the Spirit, surely the congregation would increasingly delight to 'feed on him in thy heart by faith with thanksgiving.' The final blessing, at the end of the Communion service – 'the blessing of God Almighty, the Father, the Son, and the Holy Ghost, be amongst you and remain with you always' is precious, both for the minister to say and for the people to hear. Further judicious words of explanation, both making use of Cranmer's liturgy and drawing on his theology (as expressed in his *Answer* to Gardiner), would help greatly. The use of separate or specific Communion services, perhaps after a morning or evening service with some form of break in between, would be another possibility.

God has given us a wonderfully visual, tangible dramatisation of the gospel in bread and wine, one in which all members of the church may fully and joyfully participate. This is a gift for the Church to treasure, as Cranmer so clearly realised. Let us make sure we do so!

---

[46] Null, *Repentance*, 26.

[47] Some evangelicals would ascribe that description to the sermon, or the singing. But we should be careful about pronouncing too dogmatically on this.

[48] I include myself as a guilty party in this!

These things constitute a particular challenge to leaders and pastors in Anglican evangelical or Reformed circles. We will no doubt have different perspectives on the usefulness of full-blown *BCP* services – whether in old or modern English – but we must find some way of ensuring that Cranmer's Trinitarian liturgy continues to be imprinted on Anglican hearts and minds. Therefore, we can be grateful for recent efforts from orthodox circles to produce modern *BCPs* which remain faithful to Cranmer's designs.[49] There is plenty of scope here for reflection on how best to use them.

A final, wider, consideration is the need for evangelical and Reformed Anglicans to carefully and graciously uphold Cranmer's doctrine of the Supper in the light of more liberal or Catholic theologies. They may bear the name Anglican but they are very far from Cranmer on this subject. Anglican theology is not a compromise or *via media* between Roman and Reformed teaching, despite the arguments of some to contrary. Nor will Cranmer allow us to descend into mere memorialism, still less into mysticism or nominalism. As we have seen, the Archbishop was thoroughly Reformed on the Lord's Supper: it is a gracious gift of Father, Son and Spirit, given to his people to nourish the faith they already have in Christ. It is not to be given to everyone without distinction or discernment (we noted earlier that Cranmer required communicants to be able to say the *Catechism*, which begins with an articulation of the Trinity).[50] This is not a lot of fuss about nothing, nor a mere quarrel over words: the very nature of the triune God's relationship to his people (and theirs to him) is expressed in the Holy Communion.

We have explored how the Trinity shaped all areas of Cranmer's doctrine. We must, therefore, continue to provide a clear, thoughtful and robust defence of historic, Reformed Anglican theology. Some 150

---

[49] For example, The Anglican Church in North America (ACNA) produced a 2019 *BCP* which is freely available online: https://bcp2019.anglicanchurch. net/index.php/downloads/. The smartphone app allows easy access to material such as the Daily Office. While no modern *BCP* can quite match the beauty and cadence of Cranmerian English, the ACNA 2019 *BCP* is generally excellent. It also restores the Athanasian Creed, left out in some previous American *BCPs*, although, perhaps confusingly, it allows for discretion regarding *filioque*. For a similar effort from the British side, see BCP2020: https://bcp2020.co.uk..

[50] See fn 30, above. Note also Cranmer's striking directive at the beginning of the *Order*: 'As many as intend to be partakers of the Holy Communion, shall signify their names to the Curate over night, or else in the morning, afore the beginning of Morning Prayer, or immediately after.'

years ago, Bishop of Liverpool J. C. Ryle recognised the importance of the Trinity to Anglican theology. In typical vein, he wrote:

> Let us mark... as we read the Articles, the strong and decided language which they use in speaking of *things which are essential to salvation*. Concerning the nature of God and the Holy Trinity... it is hard to conceive language more decided, clear, distinct, ringing and trumpet toned than that of the Thirty-nine Articles. There is no doubtfulness, or hesitancy, or faultering, or timidity, or uncertainty, or compromise about their statements. There is no attempt to gratify undecided theologians by saying, 'It is probably so,' – or, 'Perhaps it may be so,' – or, 'There are some grounds for thinking so,' – and all that sort of language which is so pleasing to what are called 'broad' Christians. Nothing of the kind! ... 'This is the Church of England's judgment,' they seem to say, and 'these are the views which every Churchman ought to hold.'[51]

Ryle was right: true Anglican doctrine is not even slightly ambiguous on these things. For Cranmer, the Trinity is – quite literally – the first article of faith. All Anglicans who truly follow in Cranmer's footsteps will strive to ensure that it remains so. It is very heartening, therefore, to read these words, referring to GAFCON's 2008 *The Jerusalem Declaration*:

> *In the name of God the Father, God the Son and God the Holy Spirit*: This trinitarian opening of The Jerusalem Declaration is not simply a formality. The God who is known and proclaimed throughout the world... is the triune God. God is not to be described, only or even principally, in terms of his activity, as Creator, for example, or Redeemer, or Sanctifier, but personally, in terms of his eternal relations: the Father, the Son, and the Spirit of the Father and Son.[52]

So it must remain.

---

[51] J. C. Ryle, *Knots Untied: Being Plain Statements on Disputed Points in Religion from the Standpoint of an Evangelical Churchman* (London: William Hunt & Co, 1874), 93 (emphasis original).
[52] Okoh, Samuel and Sugden, *Being Faithful*, 24–25 (italics original).

5. Conclusion

When it comes to the doctrine of the Trinity, Archbishop Thomas Cranmer's greatest legacy does not lie in a learned theological treatise (formidable scholar that he undoubtedly was), nor in any particularly novel insights or theological developments. Rather, Cranmer's outstanding contribution was to provide the English-speaking world with a truly *common* expression of the church's historic Trinitarian faith. Perhaps we may think of the *BCP* as a counterpart to Tyndale's famous Bible for the ploughboy: it is a Prayer Book for the ploughboy. Tyndale gave to English speakers the words of the triune God in our own language; Cranmer gave us words in the same language to speak in worship to the same triune God. For that, we should be very truly thankful. Where better, then, to end with the Proper Preface for Holy Communion upon the Feast of Trinity Sunday:

> It is very meet, right, and our bounden duty, that we should at all times, and in all places, give thanks to thee, O Lord, almighty and everlasting God, which art one God, one Lord, not one only person, but three persons in one substance: For that which we believe of the glory of the Father, the same we believe of the Son, and of the Holy Ghost, without any difference, or inequality. Therefore with Angels and Archangels, and with all the company of heaven, we laud and magnify thy glorious name, evermore praising thee, and saying: Holy, holy, holy, Lord God of hosts: heaven and earth are full of thy glory: glory be to thee, O Lord, most high.

Bibliography

Cranmer's works:

Bray, Gerald, ed. *Documents of the English Reformation.* Cambridge: James Clarke & Co., 1994.

————. *Tudor Church Reform: The Henrician Canons of 1535 and the Reformatio Legum Ecclesiasticarum.* Woodbridge: Boydell, 2000.

Brightman, F. E. *The English Rite: Being a Synopsis of the Sources and Revisions of the Book of Common Prayer.* 2 vols. London: Rivingtons, 1915.

Cox, John Edmund, ed. *Writings and Disputations of Thomas Cranmer, Archbishop of Canterbury, Martyr, 1556, Relative to the Sacrament of the Lord's Supper.* Cambridge: Cambridge University Press, 1844.

————. *Miscellaneous Writings and Letters of Thomas Cranmer.* Cambridge: Cambridge University Press, 1846.

Griffiths, John, ed. *The Two Books of Homilies Appointed to be Read in Churches.* Oxford: Oxford University Press, 1859.

The Book of Common Prayer, and Administration of the Sacraments, and Other Rites and Ceremonies in the Church of England. 1552. Online: http://justus.anglican.org/resources/bcp/1552/BCP_1552.htm.

Other works

Anatolios, Khaled. *Retrieving Nicaea: The Development and Meaning of Trinitarian Doctrine.* Grant Rapids, Mich.: Baker, 2011.

The Anglican Church of Canada. 'The Nicene Creed.' https://www.anglican.ca/about/beliefs/nicene-creed/.

Anglican Church in North America. 'Complete Book of Common Prayer.' https://bcp2019.anglicanchurch.net/index.php/downloads/.

The Augsburg Confession. https://bookofconcord.org/augsburg-confession/.

Ayris, Paul and David Selwyn, eds. *Thomas Cranmer: Churchman and Scholar.* Woodbridge: Boydell, 1993.

BCP2020. 'An Attempt to put the Book of Common Prayer into Common English.' https://bcp2020.co.uk.

Beeley, Christopher A. *Gregory of Nazianzus on the Trinity and the Knowledge of God: In Your Light We Shall See Light.* Oxford: Oxford University Press, 2008.

Bromiley, Geoffrey W. 'Tradition and Traditions in Thomas Cranmer.' *Anglican and Episcopal History* 59 (1990): 467–478.

Bray, Gerald. *Anglicanism: A Reformed Catholic Tradition.* Bellingham, Wash.: Lexham Press, 2021.

————. 'Filioque and Anglican-Orthodox Dialogue.' *Churchman* 93 (1979): 123–134.

————. *The Faith We Confess: An Exposition of the Thirty-Nine Articles.* London: Latimer Trust, 2009.

Chapman, Mark. *Anglican Theology.* London: T&T Clark, 2012.

The Church of England. 'What We Believe.' https://www.churchofengland.org/our-faith/what-we-believe.

The Church Pension Fund. *Enriching our Worship 1: Morning and Evening Prayer, The Great Litany, and The Holy Eucharist.* New York, N.Y.: Church Publishing, 1998.

Cottrell, Stephen. *Dear England.* London: Hodder & Stoughton, 2021.

Craig, William. 'Does Omitting the *Filioque* Clause Betray Traditional Anglican Thought?' *Anglican Theological Review* 78 (1996): 420–439.

Crowe, Brandon D., and Carl R. Trueman, eds. *The Essential Trinity: New Testament Foundations and Practical Relevance.* London: Apollos, 2016.

Cuming, G. J. *A History of Anglican Liturgy*. 2d ed. London: Macmillan, 1982.

Cummings, Brian. *The Book of Common Prayer: A Very Short Introduction*. Oxford: Oxford University Press, 2018.

Griffith Thomas, W. H. *The Principles of Theology: An Introduction to the Thirty-Nine Articles*. 6th rev. ed. London: Vine Books, 1978.

Haykin, Michael A. G. 'The Holy Spirit and Prayer in John Bunyan.' *Reformation and Revival* 3, no. 2 (Spring 1994): 85–95.

Hill, Edmund, trans. *The Works of Saint Augustine: A Translation for the 21st Century: The Trinity*. Edited by John. E. Rotelle. 2d ed. Hyde Park, N.Y.: New City Press, 2015.

House of Commons Hansard, 5 May 1813. 'Bill for the Relief of Persons Denying the Doctrine of the Trinity.' https://babel. hathitrust.org/cgi/pt?id=uc1.$b333360&view=1up&seq= 586&skin=2021.

Jensen, Michael P. *Reformation Anglican Worship: Experiencing Grace, Expressing Gratitude*. The Reformation Anglicanism Essential Library 4. Wheaton, Ill.: Crossway, 2021.

Khomami, Nadia. 'Let God be a "she", says Church of England women's group.' https://www.theguardian.com/world/2015/ jun/01/church-of-england-womens-group-bishops.

Lee, Sung Ho. 'Peter Martyr Vermigli's View of Faith and the Holy Spirit in the Eucharist.' *Reform & Revival* 23 (2019): 71–103.

Letham, Robert. *Systematic Theology*. Wheaton, Ill.: Crossway, 2019.

———. *The Holy Spirit*. Phillipsburg, N.J.: P&R, 2023.

———. *The Holy Trinity: In Scripture, Theology, History and Worship*. Rev. and enl. ed. Phillipsburg, N.J.: P&R, 2019.

———. *Through Western Eyes: Eastern Orthodoxy: A Western Perspective*. Fearn, Ross-shire: Christian Focus, 2007.

Lim, Paul C. H. *Mystery Unveiled: The Crisis of the Trinity in Early Modern England*. Oxford: Oxford University Press, 2012.

MacCulloch, Diarmaid. *Thomas Cranmer: A Life*. New Haven, Conn.: Yale University Press, 1996.

Moule, Handley, *Charles Simeon*. London: Methuen, 1892.

Needham, Nick. 'Peter Martyr and the Eucharistic Controversy.' *Scottish Bulletin of Evangelical Theology* 17 (1999): 5–25.

Null, Ashley. 'Thomas Cranmer and the Anglican Way of Reading Scripture.' *Anglican and Episcopal History* 75 (2006): 488–526.

———. *Thomas Cranmer's Doctrine of Repentance: Renewing the Power to Love*. Oxford: Oxford University Press, 2000; repr., 2010.

Null, Ashley, and John. W. Yates III., eds. *Reformation Anglicanism: A Vision for Today's Global Communion*. The Reformation Anglicanism Essential Library 1. Wheaton, Ill.: Crossway, 2017.

Okoh, Nicholas, Vinay Samuel and Chris Sugden, eds. *Being Faithful: The Shape of Historic Anglicanism Today. A Commentary on the Jerusalem Declaration Supplemented by the Way, the Truth and the Life – Theological Resources for a Pilgrimage to a Global Anglican Future*. London: Latimer Trust, 2009.

Olver, Matthew S. C. 'The Eucharistic Materials in *Enriching Our Worship 1:* A Consideration of its Trinitarian Theology.' *Anglican Theological Review* 98 (2016): 661–680.

PA Media. 'Church of England to consider use of gender-neutral terms for God.' https://www.theguardian.com/world/2023/feb/07/church-of-england-to-consider-use-of-gender-neutral-terms-for-god.

Packer, J. I. *The Gospel in the Prayer Book*. Abingdon: Marcham Manor Press, 1966.

———. 'Thomas Cranmer's Catholic Theology.' In *Honouring the People of God*. Vol. 4 of *The Collected Shorter Writings of J. I. Packer*. Carlisle: Paternoster, 1999, pp. 235–262.

Reeves, Michael. *The Good God: Enjoying Father, Son and Spirit*. Milton Keynes: Paternoster, 2012.

Rogers, Mark. '"Deliver Us from the Evil One": Martin Luther on Prayer.' *Themelios* 34 (2009): 335–347.

Ryle, J. C. *Knots Untied: Being Plain Statements on Disputed Points in Religion from the Standpoint of an Evangelical Churchman.* London: William Hunt & Co., 1874.

Sellery, David. 'We Believe in One God: Father, Son, and Holy Spirit.' *Churchman* 106 (1992): 159–162.

Selwood, Domonic. 'The British and Reading: a Short History.' https://www.bookbrunch.co.uk/page/free-article/the-british-and-reading-a-short-history/.

Starr, Chloë. 'The Prayer Book in Nineteenth-Century China.' *Monumenta Serica* 56 (2008): 395–426.

Swain, Scott R. 'The Trinity in the Reformers.' In *The Oxford Handbook of the Trinity.* Edited by Gilles Emery O.P. and Matthew Levering. Oxford: Oxford University Press, 2011, pp. 227–239.

Tan, Seng-Kong. 'The Doctrine of the Trinity in John Wesley's Prose and Poetic Works.' *Journal for Christian Theological Research* 7 (2002): 3–14.

Vermigli, Peter Martyr, *Melachim Id est, Regum Libri Duo Posteriores.* Zurich, 1566.

Wax, Trevin. 'John Stott's Morning Trinitarian Prayer.' https://www.thegospelcoalition.org/blogs/trevin-wax/john-stotts-morning-trinitarian-prayer/.

Werrell, Ralph. 'Little Known Facts About William Tyndale's Theology: The Work of the Holy Spirit and the Covenant with Man.' *Churchman* 122 (2008): 315–330.

The Westminster Confession of Faith. https://www.ligonier.org/learn/articles/the-westminster-confession-of-faith-1647.

Women and the Church. 'Liturgical Writings 2020.' https://womenandthechurch.org/resources/liturgical-writings-2020/.

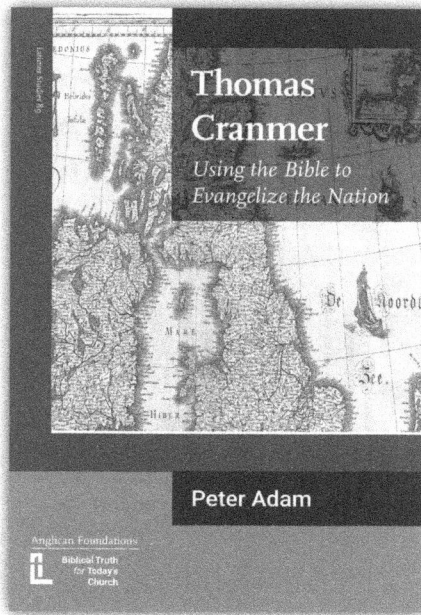

We need not only to do evangelism, but also develop contemporary gospel strategies which we trust, under God, will be effective. We need gospel wisdom, as well as gospel work. We need to work on local evangelism, but also work on God's global gospel plan. This alerts us to our own nation, as well as other nations. Gospel strategy includes the question, 'How should we evangelise our nation?' Thomas Cranmer, Archbishop of Canterbury 1532–56, strategised and worked to do this from the perspective of Anglican Reformed theology and practice. We cannot duplicate his plan in detail, but he can inspire us, and also teach us the key ingredients of such a plan.

His context of ministry had advantages and disadvantages! Our context has the same mixture. We can also learn from Cranmer's ability to work effectively in his context, despite the many problems, and the suffering he endured. God used him to evangelise his nation at his time. May God use us for his gospel glory!

Other recommendations

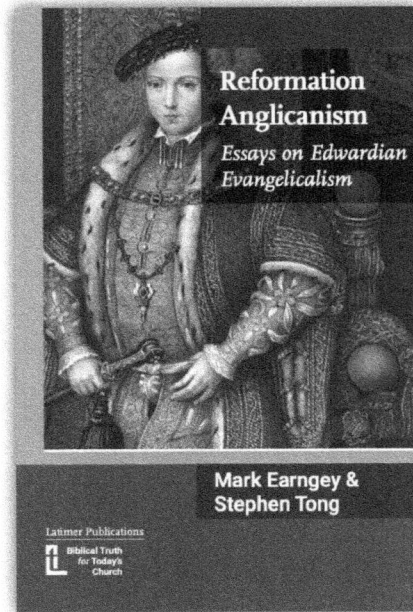

Reformation Anglicanism: Essays on Edwardian Evangelicalism is a superb set of essays arising from the Moore Theological College symposium on Reformation Anglicanism held in 2019. Featuring essays from various reformation scholars, this collection of articles focuses on some foundational documents (e.g. *Book of Homilies*, Articles of Religion) and foundational reformers (e.g. Thomas Cranmer, Martin Bucer, Heinrich Bullinger) involved with the English Reformation, and its Edwardian phase in particular. This edited volume not only offers a sustained focus on the often-neglected mid-Tudor phase of the Reformation, but explores new avenues of research on overlooked subjects such as the 45 Articles of Religion, John Ponet's *Short Catechism*, the *Reformatio Legum Ecclesiasticarum*, the ministry of John Hooper, and the memory of Martin Bucer. Students and scholars alike will benefit from this fresh examination of these anchors of Anglicanism which were hotly contested both then, and now.

In our Christian Leadership series

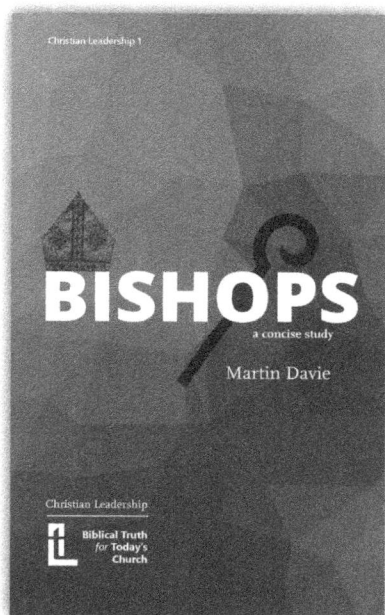

Bishops: A Concise Study summarises the key points of Martin Davie's major study *Bishops Past, Present and Future* (Gilead Books, 2022). It is designed to meet the needs of those who would like to know about the role and importance of bishops in the Church of England, but who would baulk at tackling the 800+ pages of the original book.

This concise study is published in the hope that it will help many in the Church of England, both ordained and lay, to think in a more informed fashion about how bishops should respond to the challenges and opportunities facing the Church of England at this critical point in its history.

www.ingramcontent.com/pod-product-compliance
Lightning Source LLC
Chambersburg PA
CBHW032052040426
42449CB00007B/1072